LIFE IN THE RED BRIGADE • BALLANTYNE, R. M. (ROBERT MICHAEL)

Publisher's Note

Purchase of this book entitles you to a free trial membership in the publisher's book club at www.rarebooksclub.com. (Time limited offer.) Simply enter the barcode number from the back cover onto the membership form on our home page. The book club entitles you to select from millions of books at no additional charge. You can also download a digital copy of this and related books to read on the go. Simply enter the title or subject onto the search form to find them.

Note: This is an historic book. Pages numbers, where present in the text, refer to the first edition of the book. The table of contents or index may also refer to them.

If you have any questions, could you please be so kind as to consult our Frequently Asked Questions page at www.rarebooksclub.com/faqs.cfm? You are also welcome to contact us there.

Publisher: General Books LLC™, Memphis, TN, USA, 2012. ISBN: 9781153764087.

Credits: Distributed Proofreaders.

⁂ ⁂ ⁂ ⁂ ⁂ ⁂ ⁂

R.M. Ballantyne

"Life in the Red Brigade"

Chapter One.

Wet, worn and weary—with water squeaking in his boots, and a mixture of charcoal and water streaking his face to such an extent that, as a comrade asserted, his own mother would not have known him—a stout young man walked smartly one morning through the streets of London towards his own home.

He was tall and good-looking, as well as stout, and, although wet and weary, had a spring in his step which proved beyond all question that he was not worn-out. As the comrade above referred to would have said, "there was plenty of go in him still." His blue and belted coat, sailor's cap, and small hatchet, with the brass helmet swinging by its chin strap on his left arm, betokened him a member of "The Red Brigade,"—a London fireman—one of those dare-anything characters who appear to hold their lives remarkably cheap, for they carry these lives in their hands, as the saying goes, night and day; who seem to be able to live in smoke as if it were their native element; who face the flames as if their bodies were made of cast iron; and whose apparent delight in fire is such that one is led to suspect they must be all more or less distantly connected with the family of Salamander.

The young man's expression of countenance, as far as it could be discerned through the charcoal and water, was hearty, and his name—Dashwood—was in keeping with his profession. The comrade, whose opinion we have already quoted, was wont to say that he ought to change it to Dashwater, that being his chief occupation in life. We need scarcely say that this comrade was rather fond of his joke.

Arrived at a small street, not far from the Regent Circus, young Dashwood entered a fire-station there, and found the comrade above referred to in the act of disposing himself on a narrow tressel-bed, on which there was no bedding save one blanket. The comrade happened to be on duty that night. It was his duty to repose on the tressel-bedstead, booted and belted, ready at a moment's notice to respond to "calls." Another fireman lay sleeping at his side, on another tressel-bed, similarly clothed, for there were always two men on duty all night at that station. The guard-room, or, as it was styled, the "lobby," in which they lay, was a very small room, with a bright fire in the grate, for it was winter; a plain wooden desk near the window; a plain deal table near the door, on which stood four telegraphic instruments; and having the walls ornamented with a row of Wellington boots on one side, and a row of bright brass helmets on the other, each helmet having a small hatchet suspended by a belt below it.

The comrade, who looked very sleepy, glanced at a small clock, whose tick was the only sound that fell upon the ear, and whose hands indicated the hour of half-past two.

On hearing the door open, the comrade, whose name was Bob Clazie, raised himself on one elbow.

"Ah, Joe,—that you?" he said, with a somewhat violent yawn.

"All that's left of me, anyhow," replied Joe Dashwood, as he hung up his helmet and axe on his own particular peg. "Bin much doin', Bob?"

"Not much," growled Bob; "but they don't give a poor fellow much chance of a sleep with them telegraphs. Roused me four times already within the last hour—stops for chimbleys."

"Ha! very inconsiderate of 'em," said Dashwood, turning towards the door. "It's time I had a snooze now, so I'll bid 'ee good night, Bob."

Just as he spoke, one of the sharp little telegraphic bells rang viciously. He waited to ascertain the result while Clazie rose—quickly but not hurriedly—and went to read the instrument with sleepy eyes.

"Another stop for a chimbley," he muttered, with a remonstrative growl. By this he meant that the head office in Watling Street had telegraphed that a chimney had gone on fire in some part of London; that it was being looked after, and that he and his comrades were to *stop* where they were and pay no attention to it, even although some one should rush into the office like a maniac shouting that there was a fire in that particular place. This use of the telegraph in thus *stopping* the men of the Brigade from going out in force to trifling fires, is of the greatest service, because it not only prevents them from being harassed, the engines from being horsed, and steam got up needlessly, but it prevents rascals from running from station to station, and getting several shillings, instead of the one shilling which is due to the first intimator of any fire.

Having acknowledged the message, Bob Clazie lay down once more, gave another expostulatory grunt, and drew his blanket over him; while Joe Dashwood went home.

Joe's home consisted of a small apartment round the corner of the street, within a few seconds' run of the station. Off the small apartment there was a large closet. The small apartment was Dashwood's drawing-room, dining-room, and kitchen; the large closet was his bed-room.

Dashwood had a wife, "as tight a little craft, with as pretty a figurehead," he was wont to say, "as you could find in a day's walk through London." That was saying a good deal, but there was some truth in it. When Joe entered, intending to go to bed for the night, he found that Mary had just got up for the day. It was "washing-day," or something of that sort, with Mary, which accounted for her getting up at about three in the morning.

"Hallo, lass, up already!" exclaimed the strapping fireman as he entered the room, which was a perfect marvel of tidiness, despite washing-day.

"Yes, Joe, there's plenty to do, an' little May don't give me much time to do it," replied Mary, glancing at a crib where little May, their first-born, lay coiled up in sheets like a rosebud in snow.

Joe, having rubbed the water and charcoal from his face with a huge jack-towel, went to the wash-tub, and imprinted a hearty kiss on Mary's rosy lips, which she considerately held up for the purpose of being saluted. He was about to do the same to the rosebud, when Mary stopped him with an energetic "Don't!"

"W'y not, Molly?" asked the obedient man.

"'Cause you'll wake her up."

Thus put down, Joe seated himself humbly on a sea-chest, and began to pull off his wet boots.

"It's bin a bad fire, I think," said Mary, glancing at her husband.

"Rather. A beer-shop in Whitechapel. House of five rooms burnt out, and the roof off."

"You look tired, Joe," said Mary.

"I *am* a bit tired, but an hour's rest will put me all to rights. That's the third fire I've bin called to to-night; not that I think much about that, but the last one has bin a stiff one, an' I got a fall or two that nigh shook the wind out o' me."

"Have something to eat, Joe," said Mary, in a sympathetic tone.

"No thankee, lass; I need sleep more than meat just now."

"A glass of beer, then," urged Mary, sweeping the soap suds off her pretty arms and hands, and taking up a towel.

The fireman shook his head, as he divested himself of his coat and neckcloth.

"Do, Joe," entreated Mary; "I'm sure it will do you good, and no one could say that you broke through your principles, considerin' the condition you're in."

Foolish Mary! she was young and inexperienced, and knew not the danger of tempting her husband to drink. She only knew that hundreds of first-rate, sober, good, trustworthy men took a glass of beer now and then without any evil result following, and did not think that her Joe ran the slightest risk in doing the same. But Joe knew his danger. His father had died a drunkard. He had listened to earnest men while they told of the bitter curse that drinking had been to thousands, that to some extent the tendency to drink was hereditary, and that, however safe some natures might be while moderately indulging, there were other natures to which moderate drinking was equivalent to getting on those rails which, running down a slight incline at first—almost a level—gradually pass over a steep descent, where brakes become powerless, and end at last in total destruction.

"I don't require beer, Molly," said Dashwood with a smile, as he retired in-to the large closet; "at my time o' life a man must be a miserable, half-alive sort o' critter, if he can't git along without Dutch courage. The sight o' your face and May's there, is better than a stiff glass o' grog to me any day. It makes me feel stronger than the stoutest man in the brigade. Good night, lass, or good mornin'. I must make the most o' my time. There's no sayin' how soon the next call may come. Seems to me as if people was settin' their houses alight on purpose to worry us."

The tones in which the last sentences were uttered, and the creaking of the bedstead indicated that the fireman was composing his massive limbs to rest, and scarcely had Mrs Dashwood resumed her washing, when his regular heavy breathing proclaimed him to be already in the land of Nod.

Quietly but steadily did Mrs Dashwood pursue her work. Neat little under-garments, and fairy-like little socks, and indescribable little articles of Lilliputian clothing of various kinds, all telling of the little rosebud in the crib, passed rapidly through Mary's nimble fingers, and came out of the tub fair as the driven snow. Soon the front of the fire-place became like a ship dressed with flags, with this difference, that the flags instead of being gay and parti-coloured, were white and suggestive of infancy and innocence. The gentle noise of washing, and the soft breathing of the sleepers, and the tiny ticking of the clock over the chimney-piece, were the only audible sounds, for London had reached its deadest hour, four o'clock. Rioters had exhausted their spirits, natural and artificial, and early risers had not begun to move.

Presently to these sounds were added another very distant sound which induced Mary to stop and listen. "A late cab," she whispered to herself. The rumbling of the late cab became more distinct, and soon proved it to be a hurried cab. To Mary's accustomed ear this raised some disagreeable idea. She cast a look of anxiety into the closet, wiped her hands quickly, and taking up a pair of dry boots which had been standing near the fire, placed them beside her husband's coat. This was barely accomplished when the hurried cab was heard to pull up at the neighbouring fire-station. Only a few seconds elapsed when racing footsteps were heard outside. Mary seized her husband's arm—

"Up, Joe, up," she cried and darted across the room, leaped on a chair, and laid violent hands on the tongue of the door-bell, thereby preventing a furious double ring from disturbing the rosebud!

At the first word "up," the bed in the closet groaned and creaked as the fireman bounded from it, and the house shook as he alighted on the floor. Next moment he appeared buttoning his braces, and winking like an owl in sunshine. One moment sufficed to pull on the right boot, another moment affixed the left. Catching up his half-dried coat with one hand, and flinging on his sailor's cap with the other, he darted from the house, thrust himself into his coat as he ran along and appeared at the station just as four of his comrades drew the fire-engine up to the door, while two others appeared with three horses, which they harnessed thereto—two abreast, one in front—with marvellous rapidity. The whole affair, from the "Up, Joe, up," of Mrs Dashwood, to the harnessing of the steeds, was accomplished in less than five minutes. By that time Joe and several of his mates stood ready belted, and armed with brass helmets on their heads, which flashed back the rays of the neighbouring street lamp and the engine lanterns.

There was wonderfully little noise or fuss, although there was so much display of promptitude and energy; the reason being that all the men were thoroughly drilled, and each had his particular duty to perform; there was, therefore, no room for orders, counter-orders, or confusion.

The moment the call was given, Bob Clazie, having received no telegraphic "stop," had at once run to ring up the men, who, like Dashwood, had been sleeping close at hand. He rang up the driver of the engine first. At the same moment his comrade on duty had run round to the stable, where the horses stood ready harnessed, and brought them out. Thus the thing was done without a moment's delay. The driver, when roused, flung on his coat and helmet, and ran to the engine. It was a steam fire-engine; that is, the pumps were worked by steam instead of by hand. The firing was ready laid, and the water kept nearly at the boiling point by means of a jet of gas. He had scarcely applied a light to the fire and turned off the gas, when four comrades ran into the shed, seized the red-painted engine, and dragged her out, as we have seen.

Much shorter time did it take to do all this than is required to describe it.

When the driver mounted his box, the others sprang on the engine. Crack! went the whip, fire flew from the paving-stones, fire poured from the furnace, the spirited steeds tore round the corner into Regent Street, and off they went to the fire, in the dark winter morning, like a monster rocket or a vision of Roman gladiators whirled away by a red fiery dragon!

Mrs Dashwood heard them go, and turned with a little sigh to her washing-tub. She was very proud of Joe, and she had good reason to be, for he was one of the best men in the Red Brigade, and, what was of more importance to her, he was one of the best husbands in the world. Perhaps this was largely owing to the fact that she was one of the best of wives! His career as a fireman had been short, but he had already become known as one of the daring men, to whom their Chief looked when some desperate service had to be performed. On several occasions he had, while in charge of the fire-escape, been the means of saving life. Upon the whole, therefore, it is not surprising that Mary was proud of her husband—almost as proud of him as she was of the little rosebud; but in regard to this she was never quite sure of the exact state of her mind.

Meditating on Joe, and giving an occasional glance at May, whose sweet upturned face seemed nothing short of angelic, Mrs Dashwood continued energetically to scrub the fairy-like habiliments, and make the soapsuds fly.

Meanwhile, the red engine whirled along its fiery course at full gallop, like a horrible meteor, clattering loudly in the deserted streets of the great city. So it would have sped in its wild career even if it had been broad day, for the loss of a single moment in reaching a fire is important; but in this case the men, instead of sitting like brazen-headed statues, would have stood up and increased the din of their progress by shouting continuously to clear the crowded thoroughfares. As it was, they had it all to themselves. Sometimes the corner of a window-blind was hastily lifted, showing that some wakeful one had curiosity enough to leap out of bed to see them pass. Here and there a policeman paused, and followed them with his eye as long as the tail of sparks from the furnace was visible. Occasionally a belated toper stopped in his staggering progress to gaze at them, with an idiotical assumption of seriousness and demand, "Wash ey maki'n sh' a 'orrible row for?" Now and then a cat, with exploratory tendencies, put up its back and greeted them with a glare and a fuff, or a shut-out cur gave them a yelping salute; but the great mass of the London population let them go by without notice, as they would have treated any other passing thunderbolt with which they had nothing to do.

And yet they *had* something to do with that engine, or, rather, it had to do with them. But for it, and the rest of the Red Brigade, London would have long ago been in ashes. It is only by unremitting vigilance and incessant action that the London fires can be kept within bounds. There are nearly two thousand fires in the year in the metropolis, and the heroic little army which keeps these in check numbers only three hundred and seventy-eight men. That this force is much too small for the work to be done is proved by the fact, that the same men have sometimes to turn out three, four or five times in a night, to work of the most trying and dangerous nature. There is no occupation in which the lives of the men employed are so frequently risked, and their physical endurance so severely tried, as that of a London fireman. As there are, on the average, five fires every night all the year round, it follows that he is liable to be called out several times every night; and, in point of fact, this actually takes place very often. Sometimes he has barely returned from a fire, and put off his drenched garments, when he receives another "call," and is obliged to put them on again, and go forth weary—it may be fasting—to engage in another skirmish with the flames. In all weathers and at all seasons—hot or cold, wet or dry—he must turn out at a moment's notice, to find himself, almost before he is well awake, in the midst of stifling smoke, obliged to face and to endure the power of roasting flames, to stand under cataracts of water, beside tottering walls and gables, or to plunge through smoke and flames, in order to rescue human lives. Liability to be called *occasionally* to the exercise of such courage and endurance is severe enough; it is what every soldier is liable to in time of war, and the lifeboat-man in times of storm; but to be liable to such calls several times every day and night all round the year is hard indeed, and proves that the Red Brigade, although almost perfect in its organisation and heroic in its elements, is far too small. Paris has about seven hundred fires a year; New York somewhere about three hundred; yet these cities have a far larger body of firemen than London, which with little short of two thousand fires a year, does her work of extinction with only three hundred and seventy-eight men!

She succeeds because every man in the little army is a hero, not one whit behind the Spartans of old. The London fireman, Ford, who, in 1871, at one great fire rescued six lives from the flames, and perished in accomplishing the noble deed, is a sample of the rest. All the men of the Brigade are picked men—picked from among the strapping and youthful tars of the navy, because such men are accustomed to strict discipline; to being "turned out" at all hours and in all weathers, and to climb with cool heads in trying circumstances, besides being, as a class, pre-eminently noted for daring anything and sticking at nothing. Such men are sure to do their work well, however hard; to do it without complaining, and to die, if need be, in the doing of it. But ought they to be asked to sacrifice so much? Surely Londoners would do well to make that complaint, which the men will *never* make, and insist on the force being increased, not only for the sake of the men, but also for the sake of themselves; for, although there *are* three hundred and seventy-eight heroes who hold the fiery foe so well in check, there are limits to heroic powers of action, and it stands to reason that double the number would do it better.

But we are wandering from our point. The engine has been tearing all this time at racing speed along the Bayswater Road. It turns sharp round a corner near Notting Hill Gate—so sharp that the feat is performed on the two off wheels, and draws from Bob Clazie the quiet remark, "Pretty nigh on our beam-ends that time, Joe." A light is now seen glaring in the sky over the house-tops; another moment, and the engine dashes into Ladbroke Square, where a splendid mansion is in a blaze, with the flames spouting from the windows of the second floor.

The engine pulls up with a crash; the reeking horses are removed and led aside. "Look alive, lads!" is the only word uttered, and the helmeted heroes, knowing their work well, go into action with that cool promptitude which is more than half the battle in attacking the most desperate odds or the fiercest foe.

Chapter Two.

The house on fire was, as we have said, an elegant mansion—one of those imposing edifices, with fresh paint outside, and splendid furniture within, which impress the beholder with the idea of a family in luxurious circumstances.

No one could tell how the fire originated. In the daily "report" of fires, made next day by the chief of the Red Brigade, wherein nine fires were set down as having occurred within the twenty-four hours, the cause of this fire in Ladbroke Square was reported "unknown." Of the other eight, the supposed causes were, in one case, "escape of gas," in another, "paraffin-lamp upset," in another "intoxication," in another, "spark from fire," in another, "candle," in another, "children playing with matches," and so on; but in this mansion none of these causes were deemed probable. The master of the house turned off the gas regularly every night before going to bed, therefore it could not have been caused by escape of gas. Paraffin-lamps were not used in the house. Candles were; but they were always carefully handled and guarded. As to intoxication, the most suspicious of mortals could not have dreamed of such a cause in so highly respectable a family. The fires were invariably put out at night, and guards put on in every room, therefore, no spark could have been so audacious as to have leaped into being and on to the floor. There were, indeed, "matches" in the house, but there were no children, except one old lady, who, having reached her second childhood, might perhaps have been regarded as a child. It is true there was a certain Betty, a housemaid, whose fingers were reported by the cook to be "all thumbs," and who had an awkward and incurable tendency to spill, and break, and drop, and fall over things, on whom suspicion fastened very keenly at first; but Betty, who was young and rather pretty, asserted so earnestly that she had been unusually happy that night in having done nothing whatever of a condemnable nature, and backed her asseverations with such floods of tears, that she was exonerated, and, as we have said, the cause was reported "unknown."

It was not, however, so completely unknown as was at first supposed. There was a certain grave, retiring, modest individual who knew the gentleman of the house and his doings a little more thoroughly than was agreeable to the said gentleman, and who had become aware, in some unaccountable way, which it is impossible to explain, that he, the said gentleman, had very recently furnished the house in a sumptuous style, and had insured it much beyond its value. The said individual's knowledge ultimately resulted in the said gentleman being convicted and transported for arson!

But with all this we have nothing to do. Whatever the uncertainty that afterwards arose as to the cause of the fire, there could be no uncertainty as to the fire itself at the time. It blazed and roared so furiously, that the inside of the house resembled a white-hot furnace. Flames spouted from the windows and chimneys, glaring fiercely on the spectators, who assembled rapidly from all quarters, as if defying them all, and daring the firemen to do their worst. Sparks enough to have shamed all the Roman candles ever made in or out of Rome were vomited forth continuously, and whirled away with volumes of dense black smoke into the wintry sky.

"It's well alight," observed a chimney-sweep to a policeman.

The policeman made no reply, although it did seem as if it would have been quite safe, even for a policeman, to admit that the sweep was thoroughly correct. It *was* "well alight," so well, that it seemed absolutely ridiculous to suppose that the firemen could make any impression on it at all.

But the firemen did not appear to think the attempt ridiculous. "Never give in" was, or might have been, their motto. It was their maxim to attack the enemy with promptitude and vigour, no matter what his strength might be. When he crept out like a sneaking burglar from under a hearth-stone, or through an over-heated flue, they would "have at him" with the hand-pumps and quench him at once. When he came forth like a dashing party of skirmishers, to devastate a wood-yard, or light up a music-hall with unusual brilliancy, they sent an engine or two against him without delay, and put him down in an hour or two. When he attacked "in force," they despatched engine after engine—manuals and steamers—to the front, until he was quelled, and if the prey already seized could not be wrenched from his grasp, they, at all events, killed him before he could destroy more. When he boldly and openly declared war, attacking the great combustible warehouses of Tooley Street, threatening a descent on the shipping, and almost setting the Thames on fire, they sent out the whole available army from every quarter of the metropolis with all their engines of war—manuals, steamers, and floating batteries, or spouteries, and fought him tooth and nail, till he gave in. They might be terribly over-matched—as in the case of the great fire when the gallant Braidwood fell—they might lose men, and might have to fight day and night for weeks, but they would "never say die," until the enemy had died and left them, tired and torn, but still tough and triumphant victors on the field of battle.

Before the engine from Regent Street came on the ground, two manual engines from Kensington and Notting Hill had arrived, and opened water on the foe. At first their shot fell harmlessly on the roaring furnace; but by the time the "steamer" had got ready for action, some little effect was beginning to be produced. When this great gun, so to speak, began to play, and sent a thick continuous stream through the windows, like an inexhaustible water mitrailleuse, clouds of white steam mingled with the black smoke, and varied the aspect of the fire, but did not appear to lessen its fury in any degree. Just then another manual engine dashed into the square at full gallop, and formed up. Before it had well taken a position, another "steamer," with three horses, came swinging round the corner, and fell into the ranks. The panting steeds were unharnessed, the bold charioteers leaped down, the suction-pipe was dipped into the water-trough, and the hose attached. As two engines cannot "drink" at the same plug, a canvas trough with an iron frame is put over the plug, having a hole in its bottom, which fits tightly round the plug. It quietly fills, and thus two or more engines may do their work convivially—dip in their suction-pipes, and "drink" simultaneously at the same fountain.

"Down with her!" shouted the man who held the "branch," or nozzle, at the end of the hose.

A steam whistle gives a shrill, short reply; the engine quivers under the power of man's greatest servant, and another battery opens on the foe.

But London firemen are not content to play at long bowls. While the artillery goes thus vigorously into action, the helmets of the men are seen gleaming and glancing everywhere amid the smoke, searching for weak points, turning the enemy's flanks, and taking him in rear. Hose are dragged through neighbouring houses, trailing their black coils like horrid water snakes, through places were such things were never meant to be. If too short, additional lengths are added, again and again, till the men who hold the branches gain points of vantage on adjoining roofs or outhouses, until, at last from below, above, in front, and behind, cataracts of water dash into the glowing furnace.

The fire-escape had been first to reach the ground after the alarm was given, this being the instrument nearest to the scene of conflagration. It happened that night to be in charge of David Clazie, a brother of Comrade Bob. Being a smart young fellow, David, had—with the assistance of two early risers who chanced to be at hand, and the policeman on the beat—run up his escape, and put it in position before the fire had gained its full force. The gentleman of the house had already got out, and fled in his night garments; but the fire had rendered the staircase impassable, so that the cook, the many-thumbed Betty, and the old lady, who was the gentleman's mother, were imprisoned in the upper floor.

David Clazie did not learn this from the gentleman, however. That amiable character had received such a fright, that he had taken himself off, no one—except the individual aforementioned—knew whither. Fortunately, Betty announced the fact of her existence by rushing to a window and shrieking. David ran his escape towards the window, mounted the ladder, carried the damsel down, bore her, kicking, into a neighbouring house, and left her in fits. Meanwhile the cook rushed to the same window, shrieked, and fell back half-suffocated with the smoke which just then surrounded her. A policeman gallantly ran up the escape, jumped into the room, gathered up the cook with great difficulty—for she was unusually fat and the smoke very suffocating—carried her down, bore her to the same house where Betty lay, and left her there in violent hysterics.

As neither of them could answer questions, it could not be ascertained whether there were any more people in the burning house. David therefore explored it as far as was possible in the circumstances, and much more than was safe for himself, but found no one. After nearly choking himself, therefore, he drew aside the escape to prevent its being burned.

When the engines came up, however, it was again brought into play, to enable the firemen to get up with their "branches" to the upper windows.

"Try that window, Dashwood," said the officer of the station to which Joe belonged, pointing to a window on the second floor. "There ain't much smoke coming out."

Before he had done speaking, Joe and a comrade had pushed the escape towards the window in question. He ascended and leaped into the room, but could scarcely see for the smoke. Knowing that the air in a burning house is clearer near the floor, he stooped as low as possible, and went round the room guiding himself by the walls. Coming to a door he seized the handle and tried to open it, but found it locked, and the handle so hot that he was forced to let go abruptly. He seized a chair, tried to burst it open with a blow, and shivered the chair to atoms, but did not force the door. A powerful effort with his foot also failed. Rushing to the window he got out on the escape, and shouted:—

"The axe, lads, look sharp and pass up the hose. We'll get at it here."

A large heavy axe was handed up by one fireman, while another let down a rope, to which the end of the hose was attached and hauled up.

Joe seized the axe, returned to the door, and, with one blow, dashed it open.

Flames leaped upon him, as if they had been eagerly awaiting the opportunity, licked hungrily round his legs, and kissed his whiskers—of which, by the way, he was rather proud; and with good reason, for they were very handsome whiskers. But Joe cared no more for them at that moment than he did for his boots. He was forced to retreat, however, to the window, where Bob Clazie had already presented his branch and commenced a telling discharge on the fire.

"That's the way to do it," muttered Bob, as he directed the branch and turned aside his head to avoid, as much as possible, the full volume of the smoke.

"Let's get a breath o' fresh air," gasped Joe Dashwood, endeavouring to squeeze past his comrade through the window.

At that moment a faint cry was heard. It appeared to come from an inner room.

"Some one there, Joe," said Bob Clazie in a grave tone, but without diverting his attention for an instant from the duty in which he was engaged.

Joe made no reply, but at once leaped back into the room, and, a second time, felt his way round the walls. He came on another door. One blow of the ponderous axe dashed it in, and revealed a bed-room not quite so densely filled with smoke as the outer room. Observing a bed looming through the smoke, he ran towards it, and struck his head against one of the posts so violently that he staggered. Recovering he made a grasp at the clothes, and felt that there was a human being wrapped tightly up in them like a bundle. A female shriek followed. Joe Dashwood was not the man to stand on ceremony in such circumstances. He seized the bundle, straightened it out a little, so as to make it more portable, and throwing it over his shoulder, made a rush towards the window by which he had entered. All this the young fireman did with considerable energy and haste, because the density of the smoke was increasing, and his retreat might be cut off by the flames at any moment.

"Clear the way there!" he gasped, on reaching the window.

"All right," replied Bob Clazie, who was still presenting his branch with untiring energy at the flames.

Joe passed out, got on the head of the escape, and, holding the bundle on his shoulder with one hand, grasped the rounds of the ladder with the other. He descended amid the cheers of the vast multitude, which had by this time assembled to witness the fire.

As Joe hurried towards the open door of the nearest house, Betty, with the thumbs, rushed frantically out, screaming, "Missis! oh! my! she'll be burnt alive! gracious! help! fire! back room! first floor! oh, my!"

"Be easy, lass," cried Joe, catching the flying domestic firmly by the arm, and detaining her despite her struggles.

"Let me go; missis! I forgot her!"

"Here she is," cried Joe, interrupting, "all safe. You come and attend to her."

The reaction on poor Betty's feelings was so great that she went into fits a second time, and was carried with her mistress into the house, where the cook still lay in violent hysterics.

Joe laid the bundle gently on the bed, and looked quickly at the bystanders. Observing several cool and collected females among them, he pointed to the bundle, which had begun to exhibit symptoms of life, and said briefly, "She's all right, look after her," and vanished like a wreath of that smoke into which in another moment he plunged.

He was not a moment too soon, for he found Bob Clazie, despite his fortitude and resolution, on the point of abandoning the window, where the smoke had increased to such a degree as to render suffocation imminent.

"Can't stand it," gasped Bob, scrambling a few paces down the ladder.

"Give us the branch, Bob, I saw where it was in fetchin' out the old woman," said Joe in a stifled voice.

He grasped the copper tube from which the water spouted with such force as to cause it to quiver and recoil like a living thing, so that, being difficult to hold, it slipped aside and nearly fell. The misdirected water-spout went straight at the helmet of a policeman, which it knocked off with the apparent force of a cannon shot; plunged into the bosom of a stout collier, whom it washed whiter than he had ever been since the days of infancy, and scattered the multitude like chaff before the wind. Seeing this, the foreman ordered "Number 3" engine, (which supplied the particular branch in question), to cease pumping.

Joe recovered the erratic branch in a moment, and dragged it up the escape, Bob, who was now in a breatheable atmosphere, helping to pass up the hose. The foreman, who seemed to have acquired the power of being in several places at one and the same moment of time, and whose watchful eye was apparently everywhere, ordered Bob's brother David and another man named Ned Crashington, to go up and look after Joe Dashwood.

Meanwhile Joe shouted, "Down with Number 3;" by which he meant, "up with as much water as possible from Number 3, and as fast as you can!" and sprang into the room from which he had just rescued the old woman. In passing out with her he had observed a glimmer of flame through the door which he had first broken open, and which, he reflected while descending the escape, was just out of range of Bob Clazie's branch. It was the thought of this that had induced him to hurry back so promptly; in time, as we have seen, to relieve his comrade. He now pointed the branch at the precise spot, and hit that part of the fire right in its heart. The result was that clouds of steam mingled with the smoke. But Joe was human after all. The atmosphere, or, rather, the want of atmosphere, was too much for him. He was on the point of dropping the branch, and rushing to the window for his life, when Ned Crashington, feeling his way into the room, tumbled over him.

Speech was not required in the circumstances. Ned knew exactly what to do, and Joe knew that he had been sent to relieve him. He therefore delivered the branch to Ned, and at once sprang out on the escape, where he encountered David Clazie.

"Go in, Davy, he can't stand it long," gasped Joe.

"No fears of 'im," replied Davy, with a smile, as he prepared to enter the window; "Ned can stand hanythink a'most. But, I say, send up some more 'ands. It takes two on us to 'old *that* 'ere branch, you know."

The brass helmets of more hands coming up the escape were observed as he spoke, for the foreman saw that this was a point of danger, and, like a wise general, had his reserves up in time.

David Clazie found Ned standing manfully to the branch. Ned was noted in the Red Brigade as a man who could "stand a'most anything," and who appeared to cherish a martyr-like desire to die by roasting or suffocation. This was the more surprising that he was not a boastful or excitable fellow, but a silent, melancholy, and stern man, who, except when in action, usually seemed to wish to avoid observation. Most of his comrades were puzzled by this compound of character, but some of them hinted that Crashington's wife could have thrown some light on the subject. Be this as it may, whenever the chief or the foreman of the Brigade wanted a man for any desperate work, they invariably turned to Ned Crashington. Not that Ned was one whit more courageous or willing to risk his life than any of the other men, *all* of whom, it must be remembered, were picked for courage and capacity for their special work; but he combined the greatest amount of coolness with the utmost possible recklessness, besides being unusually powerful, so that he could be depended on for wise as well as desperate action. Joe Dashwood was thought to be almost equal to Ned—indeed, in personal activity he was superior; but there was nothing desperate in Joe's character. He was ever ready to dare anything with a sort of jovial alacrity, but he did not appear, like Ned, to court martyrdom.

While Ned and David subdued the flames above, Joe descended the escape, and being by that time almost exhausted, sat down to rest with several comrades who had endured the first shock of battle, while fresh men were sent to continue the fight.

"Have a glass, Joe?" said one of the firemen, coming round with a bottle of brandy.

"No, thank 'ee," said Joe, "I don't require it."

"Hand it here," said a man who stood leaning against the rails beside him, "my constitution is good, like the British one, but it's none the worse for a drop o' brandy after such tough work."

There was probably truth in what the man said. Desperate work sometimes necessitates a stimulant; nevertheless, there were men in the Red Brigade who did their desperate work on nothing stronger than water, and Joe was one of these.

In three hours the fire was subdued, and before noon of that day it was extinguished. The "report" of it, as published by the chief of the Fire-Brigade next morning, recorded that a house in Ladbroke Square, occupied by Mr Blank, a gentleman whose business was "private"—in other words, unknown—had been set on fire by some "unknown cause," that the whole tenement had been "burnt out" and "the roof off," and that the contents of the building were "insured in the Phoenix."

Some of the firemen were sent home about daybreak, when the flames first began to be mastered.

Joe was among these. He found Mary ready with a cup of hot coffee, and the rosebud, who had just awakened, ready with a kiss. Joe accepted the second, swallowed the first, stretched his huge frame with a sigh of weariness, remarked to Mary that he would turn in, and in five minutes thereafter was snoring profoundly.

Chapter Three.

One pleasant afternoon in spring David Clazie and Ned Crashington sat smoking together in front of the fire in the lobby of the station, chatting of hair-breadth escapes by flood and fire.

"It's cold enough yet to make a fire a very pleasant comrade—w'en 'e's inside the bars," observed David.

"H'm," replied Crashington.

As this was not a satisfactory reply, David said so, and remarked, further, that Ned seemed to be in the blues.

"Wotever can be the matter wi' you, Ned," said David, looking at his companion with a perplexed air; "you're a young, smart, 'ealthy fellar, in a business quite to your mind, an' with a good-lookin' young wife at 'ome, not to mention a babby. W'y wot more would you 'ave, Ned? You didn't ought for to look blue."

"Pr'aps not," replied Ned, re-lighting his pipe, and puffing between sentences, "but a man may be in a business quite to his mind and have a good-looking wife, and a babby, and health to boot, without bein' exactly safe from an attack of the blues now and then, d'ye see? 'It ain't all gold that glitters.' You've heard o' that proverb, no doubt?"

"Well, yes," replied Clazie.

"Ah. Then there's another sayin' which mayhap you've heard of too: 'every man's got a skeleton in the cupboard.'"

"I've heard o' that likewise," said Clazie, "but it ain't true; leastways, *I* have got no skeleton in none o' my cupboards, an', wot's more, if I 'ad, I'd pitch him overboard."

"But what if he was too strong for you?" suggested Ned.

"Why, then—I don't know," said Clazie, shaking his head.

Before this knotty point could be settled in a satisfactory manner, the comrades were interrupted by the entrance of a man. He was a thick-set, ill-favoured fellow, with garments of a disreputable appearance, and had a slouch that induced honest men to avoid his company. Nevertheless, Ned Crashington gave him a hearty "good afternoon," and shook hands.

"My brother-in-law, Clazie," said Ned, turning and introducing him, "Mr Sparks."

Clazie was about to say he "was 'appy to," etcetera, but thought better of it, and merely nodded as he turned to the grate and shook the ashes out of his pipe.

"You'll come and have a cup of tea, Phil? Maggie and I usually have it about this time."

Phil Sparks said he had no objection to tea, and left the station with Ned, leaving David Clazie shaking his head with a look of profound wisdom.

"You're a bad lot, you are," growled David, after the man was gone, "a werry bad lot, indeed!"

Having expressed his opinion to the clock, for there was no one else present, David thrust both hands into his pockets, and went out to take an observation of the weather.

Meanwhile Ned Crashington led his brother-in-law to his residence, which, like the abodes of the other firemen, was close at hand. Entering it he found his "skeleton" waiting for him in the shape of his wife. She was anything but a skeleton in aspect, being a stout, handsome woman, with a fine figure, an aquiline nose, and glittering black eyes.

"Oh, you've come at last," she said in a sharp, querulous tone, almost before her husband had entered the room. "Full ten minutes late, and I expected you sooner than usual to-night."

"I didn't know you expected me sooner, Maggie. Here's Phil come to have tea with us."

"Oh, Phil, how are you?" said Mrs Crashington, greeting her brother with a smile, and shaking him heartily by the hand.

"Ah, if you'd only receive *me* with a smile like that, *how* different it might be," thought Ned; but he *said* nothing.

"Now, then, stoopid," cried Mrs Crashington, turning quickly round on her husband, as if to counteract the little touch of amiability into which she had been betrayed, "how long are you going to stand there in people's way staring at the fire? What are you thinking of?"

"I was thinking of you, Maggie."

"H'm! thinking no good of me, I dare say," replied Maggie, sharply.

"Did your conscience tell you that?" asked Ned, with a heightened colour.

Maggie made no reply. One secret of her bad temper was that she had all her life been allowed to vent it, and now that she was married she felt the necessity of restraining it very irksome. Whenever she had gone far enough with Ned, and saw that he was not to be trifled with, she found that she possessed not only power to control her temper, but the sense, now and then, to do so! On the present occasion she at once busied herself in preparing tea, while Ned sat down opposite his brother-in-law, and, taking Fred, his only child, a handsome boy of about five years of age, on his knee, began to run his fingers through his jet black curly hair.

"Did you get your tasks well to-day, Fred?" asked Ned.

"No, father."

"No?" repeated Ned in surprise; "why not?"

"Because I was playin' with May Dashwood, father."

"Was that a good reason for neglecting your dooty?" demanded Ned, shaking his head reproachfully, yet smiling in spite of himself.

"Iss, father," replied the boy boldly.

"You're wrong, Fred. No doubt you might have had a worse reason, but *play* is not a good reason for neglect of dooty. Only think—what would be said to me if I was called to a fire, and didn't go because I wanted to play with May Dashwood?"

"But I was sent for," pleaded Fred. "Mrs Dashwood had a big—oh, *such* a big washin', an' sent to say if I might be let go; an' mother said I might, so I went."

"Ah, that alters the case, Fred," replied his father, patting the boy's head. "To help a woman in difficulties justifies a'most anything. Don't it, Phil?"

Thus appealed to, Phil said that he didn't know, and, what was more, he didn't care.

"Now don't sit talkin' nonsense, but sit in to tea," said Mrs Crashington.

The stout fireman's natural amiability had been returning like a flood while he conversed with Fred, but this sharp summons rather checked its flow; and when he was told in an exasperating tone to hand the toast, and not look like a stuck pig, it was fairly stopped, and his spirit sank to zero.

"Have you got anything to do yet?" he asked of Phil Sparks, by way of cheering up a little.

"No, nothin'," replied Sparks; "leastways nothin' worth mentionin'."

"I *knew* his last application would fail," observed Maggie, in a quietly contemptuous tone.

His last application had been made through Ned's influence and advice, and that is how she came to *know* it would fail.

Ned felt a rising of indignation within him which he found it difficult to choke down, because it was solely for his wife's sake that he had made any effort at all to give a helping hand to surly Phil Sparks, for whom he entertained no personal regard. But Ned managed to keep his mouth shut. Although a passionate man, he was not ill-tempered, and often suffered a great deal for the sake of peace.

"London," growled Sparks, in a tone of sulky remonstrance, "ain't a place for a man to git on in. If you've the luck to have friends who can help you, an' are willin', why it's well enough; but if you haven't got friends, its o' no manner o' use to try anything, except pocket-pickin' or house-breakin'."

"Come, Phil," said Ned, laughing, as he helped himself to a huge round of buttered toast, "I 'ope you han't made up your mind to go in for either of them professions, for they don't pay. They entail hard work, small profits, an' great risk—not to mention the dishonesty of 'em. But I don't agree with you about London neither."

"You never agree with nobody about anythink," observed Mrs Crashington, in a low tone, as if the remark were made to the teapot; but Ned heard it, and his temper was sorely tried again, for, while the remark was utterly false as regarded himself, it was particularly true as regarded his wife. However, he let it pass, and continued—

"You see, Phil, London, as you know, is a big place, the population of it being equal to that of all Scotland—so I'm told, though it ain't easy to swallow that. Now it seems to me that where there's so many people an' so much doin', it ought to be the very place for smart, stout fellows like you. If I was you, I'd—"

"Yes, but you *ain't* him," interrupted Mrs Crashington, testily, "so it won't do him much good to tell what you would or wouldn't do."

"I've heard of wives, Maggie, who *sometimes* tried to be agreeable," said Ned, gravely.

"If I don't suit you, why did you marry me?" demanded Maggie.

"Ah, why indeed?" said Ned, with a frown. At this critical point in the conversation, little Fred, who was afraid that a storm was on the point of bursting forth, chanced to overturn his tin mug of tea. His mother was one of those obtuse women who regard an accident as a sin, to be visited by summary punishment. Her usual method of inflicting punishment was by means of an open-handed slap on the side of the head. On this occasion she dealt out the measure of justice with such good-will, that poor little Fred was sent sprawling and howling on the floor.

This was too much for Ned, who was a tender-hearted man. The blood rushed to his face; he sprang up with such violence as to overturn his chair, seized his cap, and, without uttering a word, dashed out of the room, and went downstairs three steps at a time.

What Ned meant to do, or where to go, of course no one could tell, for he had no definite intentions in his own mind, but his energies were unexpectedly directed for him. On rushing out at the street door, he found himself staggering unexpectedly in the arms of Bob Clazie.

"Hullo! Bob, what's up?"

"Turn out!" said Bob, as he wheeled round, and ran to the next fireman's door.

Ned understood him. He ran smartly to the station, and quickly put on helmet, belt, and axe. Already the engine was out, and the horses were being harnessed. In two minutes the men were assembled and accoutred; in three they were in their places—the whip cracked, and away they went.

It was a good blazing, roaring, soul-stirring fire—a dry-salter's warehouse, with lots of inflammable materials to give it an intense heart of heat, and fanned by a pretty stiff breeze into ungovernable fury—yet it was as nothing to the fire that raged in Ned's bosom. If he had hated his wife, or been indifferent to her, he would in all probability, like too many husbands, have sought for congenial society elsewhere, and would have been harsh to her when obliged to be at home. But Ned loved his wife, and would have made any sacrifice, if by so doing, he could have smoothed her into a more congenial spirit. When, therefore, he found that his utmost efforts were of no avail, and that he was perpetually goaded, and twitted, and tweaked for every little trifle, his spirit was set alight—as he at last remarked in confidence to David Clazie—and all the fire-engines in Europe, Asia, Africa and America couldn't put it out.

The dry-salter's premises seemed to have been set on fire for poor Ned's special benefit that night. They suited his case exactly. There was more than the usual quantity of smoke to suffocate, and fire to roast, him. There was considerable danger too, so that the daring men of the brigade were in request—if we may say that of a brigade in which *all* the men were daring—and Ned had congenial work given him to do. The proverbial meeting of Greek with Greek was mere child's play to this meeting of fire with fire. The inflamed Ned and the blazing dry-salter met in mortal conflict, and the result was tremendous! It made his brother firemen stand aghast with awful admiration, to observe the way in which Ned dashed up tottering staircases, and along smoke-choked passages, where lambent flames were licking about in search of oxygen to feed on, and the way in which he hurled down brick walls and hacked through wood partitions, and tore up fir-planking and seized branch and hose, and, dragging them into hole-and-corner places, and out upon dizzy beams, and ridge poles, dashed tons of water in the fire's face, until it hissed again. It was a fine example of the homoeopathic principle that "like cures like;" for the fire in Ned's bosom did wonders that night in the way of quenching the fire in the dry-salter's warehouse.

When this had gone on for an hour,

and the fire was at its height, Ned, quite exhausted, descended to the street, and, sitting down on the pavement, leaned against a rail.

"If you goes on like that, Ned," said Bob Clazie, coming up to him, "you'll bust yourself."

"I wish I could," said Ned.

At that moment, Bob's brother David came towards them with the brandy bottle.

"Have a glass, Ned, you need it," said David.

Ned, although not a teetotaller, was one of the men who did not require spirits, and therefore seldom took more than a sip, but he now seized the glass, and drained it eagerly.

"Another," he cried, holding it up.

David refilled it with a look of some surprise.

Ned drained it a second time.

"Now," said he, springing up, and tightening his belt, "I'm all right, come along, Bob!"

With that he rushed into the burning house, and in a few seconds was seen to take the branch from a fireman on one of the upper floors, and drag it out on a charred beam that overhung the fire. The spot on which they stood was brilliantly illuminated, and it was seen that the fireman remonstrated with Ned, but the latter thrust him away, and stepped out on the beam. He stood there black as ebony, with a glowing background of red walls and fire, and the crowd cheered him for his unwonted courage; but the cheer was changed abruptly into a cry of alarm as the beam gave way, and Ned fell head foremost into the burning ruins.

The chief of the brigade—distinguishable everywhere by his tall figure—observed the accident, and sprang towards the place.

"If he's not killed by the fall, he's safe from the fire, for it is burnt out there," he remarked to David Clazie, who accompanied him. Before they reached the place, Joe Dashwood and two other men had rushed in. They found Ned lying on his back in a mixture of charcoal and water, almost buried in a mass of rubbish which the falling beam had dragged down along with it. In a few seconds this was removed, and Ned was carried out and laid on the pavement, with a coat under his head.

"There's no cut anywhere that I can see," said Joe Dashwood examining him.

"His fall must have been broke by goin' through the lath and plaster o' the ceilin' below," suggested Bob Clazie.

At that moment, there was a great crash, followed by a loud cry, and a cheer from the multitude, as the roof fell in, sending up a magnificent burst of sparks and flame, in the midst of which Ned Crashington was borne from the field of battle.

While this scene was going on, Mrs Crashington and her brother were still seated quietly enjoying their tea—at least, enjoying it as much as such characters can be said to enjoy anything.

When Ned had gone out, as before mentioned, Phil remarked:—

"I wouldn't rouse him like that, Mag, if I was you."

"But he's so aggravatin'," pleaded Mrs Crashington.

"He ain't half so aggravatin' as *you* are," replied Phil, gruffly. "I don't understand your temper at all. You take all the hard words *I* give you as meek as a lamb, but if *he* only offers to open his mouth you fly at him like a turkey-cock. However, it's no business o' mine, and now," he added, rising, "I must be off."

"So, you won't tell me before you go, what sort of employment you've got?"

"No," replied Phil, shortly.

"Why not, Phil?"

"Because I don't want you to know, and I don't want your husband to know."

"But I won't tell him, Phil."

"I'll take good care you can't tell him," returned Phil, as he fastened a worsted comforter round his hairy throat. "It's enough for you to know that I ain't starvin' and that the work pays, though it ain't likely to make my fortin'."

Saying this, Mr Sparks condescended to give his sister a brief nod and left the house.

He had not been gone much more than a couple of hours, when Mrs Crashington, having put little Fred to sleep, was roused from a reverie by the sound of several footsteps outside, followed by a loud ring at the bell; she opened the door quickly, and her husband was borne in and laid on his bed.

"Not dead?" exclaimed the woman in a voice of agony.

"No, missus, not dead," said David Clazie, "but hardly better, I fear."

When Maggie looked on the poor bruised form, with garments torn to shreds, and so covered with charcoal, water, lime, and blood, as to be almost an indistinguishable mass, she could not have persuaded herself that he was alive, had not a slight heaving of the broad chest told that life still remained.

"It's a 'orrible sight, that, missus," said David Clazie, with a look that seemed strangely stern.

"It is—oh it is—terrible!" said Mrs Crashington, scarce able to suppress a cry.

"Ah, you'd better take a good look at it," added Clazie, "for it's your own doing, missus."

Maggie looked at him in surprise, but he merely advised her to lend a hand to take the clothes off, as the doctor would be round in a minute; so she silently but actively busied herself in such duties as were necessary.

Meanwhile Phil Sparks went about the streets of London attending to the duties of his own particular business. To judge from appearances, it seemed to be rather an easy occupation, for it consisted mainly in walking at a leisurely pace through the streets and thoroughfares, with his hands in his pockets and a pipe in his mouth.

Meditation also appeared to be an important branch of this business, for Phil frequently paused in front of a large mansion, or a magnificent shop, and gazed at it so intently, that one might have almost fancied he was planning the best method of attempting a burglary, although nothing was farther from Phil's intentions. Still, his meditations were sometimes so prolonged, that more than one policeman advised him, quite in a friendly way, to "move on."

Apparently, however, Phil turned over no profit, on this business, and was about to return home supperless to bed, when he suddenly observed smoke issuing from an upper window. Rare and lucky chance! He was the first to observe it. He knew that the first who should convey the alarm of fire to a fire-station would receive a shilling for his exertions. He dashed off at once, had the firemen brought to the spot in a few minutes, so that the fire was easily and quickly overcome. Thus honest Phil Sparks earned his supper, and the right to go home and lay his head on his pillow, with the happy consciousness of having done a good action to his fellow-men, and performed a duty to the public and himself.

Chapter Four.

It is probable that there is not in all the wide world a man—no matter how depraved, or ill-favoured, or unattractive—who cannot find some sympathetic soul, some one who will be glad to see him and find more or less pleasure in his society. Coarse in body and mind though Philip Sparks was, there dwelt a young woman, in one of the poorest of the poor streets in the neighbourhood of Thames Street, who loved him, and would have laid down her life for him.

To do Martha Reading justice, she had fallen in love with Sparks before intemperance had rendered his countenance repulsive and his conduct brutal. When, perceiving the power he had over her, he was mean enough to borrow and squander the slender gains she made by the laborious work of dress-making—compared to which coal-heaving must be mere child's play—she experienced a change in her feelings towards him, which she could not easily understand or define. Her thoughts of him were mingled with intense regrets and anxieties, and she looked forward to his visits with alarm. Yet those thoughts were not the result of dying affection; she felt quite certain of that, having learned from experience that, "many waters cannot quench love."

One evening, about eight o'clock, Phil Sparks, having prosecuted his "business" up to that hour without success, tapped at the door of Martha's garret and entered without waiting for permission; indeed, his tapping at all was a rather unwonted piece of politeness.

"Come in, Phil," said Martha, rising and shaking hands, after which she resumed her work.

"You seem busy to-night," remarked Sparks, sitting down on a broken chair beside the fireless grate, and taking out his bosom companion, a short black pipe, which he began to fill.

"I am always busy," said Martha, with a sigh.

"An' it don't seem to agree with you, to judge from your looks," rejoined the man.

This was true. The poor girl's pretty face was thin and very pale and haggard.

"I was up all last night," she said, "and feel tired now, and there's not much chance of my getting to bed to-night either, because the lady for whom I am making this must have it by to-morrow afternoon at latest."

Here Mr Sparks muttered something very like a malediction on ladies in general, and on ladies who "*must*" have dresses in particular.

"Your fire's dead out, Martha," he added, poking among the ashes in search of a live ember.

"Yes, Phil, it's out. I can't afford fire of an evening; besides it ain't cold just now."

"You can afford matches, I suppose," growled Phil; "ah, here they are. Useful things matches, not only for lightin' a feller's pipe with, but also for—well; so she *must* have it by to-morrow afternoon, must she?"

"Yes, so my employer tells me."

"An' she'll not take no denial, won't she?"

"I believe not," replied Martha, with a faint smile, which, like a gleam of sunshine on a dark landscape, gave indication of the brightness that might have been if grey clouds of sorrow had not overspread her sky.

"What's the lady's name, Martha?"

"Middleton."

"And w'ere abouts may she live?"

"In Conway Street, Knightsbridge."

"The number?"

"Number 6, I believe; but why are you so particular in your inquiries about her?" said Martha, looking up for a moment from her work, while the faint gleam of sunshine again flitted over her face.

"Why, you see, Martha," replied Phil, gazing through the smoke of his pipe with a sinister smile, "it makes a feller feel koorious to hear the partiklers about a lady wot *must* have things, an' won't take no denial! If I was you, now, I'd disappoint her, an' see how she'd take it."

He wound up his remark, which was made in a bantering tone, with another malediction, which was earnest enough—savagely so.

"Oh! Phil," cried the girl, in an earnest tone of entreaty; "don't, oh, don't swear so. It is awful to think that God hears you, is near you—at your very elbow—while you thus insult Him to his face."

The man made no reply, but smoked with increasing intensity, while he frowned at the empty fire-place.

"Well, Martha," he said, after a prolonged silence, "I've got work at last."

"Have you?" cried the girl, with a look of interest.

"Yes; it ain't much to boast of, to be sure, but it pays, and, as it ties me to nothin' an' nobody, it suits my taste well. I'm wot you may call a appendage o' the fire-brigade. I hangs about the streets till I sees a fire, w'en, off I goes full split to the nearest fire-station, calls out the engine, and gits the reward for bein' first to give the alarm."

"Indeed," said Martha, whose face, which had kindled up at first with pleasure, assumed a somewhat disappointed look; "I—I fear you won't make much by that, Phil?"

"You don't seem to make much by that," retorted Phil, pointing with the bowl of his pipe to the dress which lay in her lap and streamed in a profusion of rich folds down to the floor.

"Not much," assented Martha, with a sigh. "Well, then," continued Phil, re-lighting his pipe, and pausing occasionally in his remarks to admire the bowl, "that bein' so, you and I are much in the same fix, so if we unites our small incomes, of course that'll make 'em just double the size."

"Phil," said Martha, in a lower voice, as she let her hands and the work on which they were engaged fall on her lap, "I think, now, that it will never be."

"What'll never be?" demanded the man rudely, looking at the girl in surprise.

"Our marriage."

"What! are you going to jilt me?"

"Heaven forbid," said Martha, earnestly. "But you and I are not as we once were, Phil, we differ on many points. I feel sure that our union would make us more miserable than we are."

"Come, come," cried the man, half in jest and half in earnest. "This kind of thing will never do. You mustn't joke about that, old girl, else I'll have you up for breach of promise."

Mr Sparks rose as he spoke, knocked the ashes out of his pipe, put it in his waistcoat pocket, and prepared to go.

"Martha," he said, "I'm goin' off now to attend to my business, but I haven't made a rap yet to-day, and its hard working on a empty stomach, so I just looked in to light my pipe, and enquire if you hadn't got a shillin' about you, eh!"

The girl looked troubled.

"Oh, very well," cried Sparks, with an offended air, "if you don't *want* to accommodate me, never mind, I can get it elsewhere."

"Stop!" cried Martha, taking a leathern purse from her pocket.

"Well, it *would* have been rather hard," he said, returning and holding out his hand.

"There, take it," said Martha, "You shouldn't judge too quickly. You don't know *why* I looked put out. It is my—"

She stopped short, and then said hurriedly, "Don't drink it, Phil."

"No, I won't. I'm hungry. I'll eat it. Thankee."

With a coarse laugh he left the room, and poor Martha sat down again to her weary toil, which was not in any degree lightened by the fact that she had just given away her last shilling.

A moment after, the door opened suddenly and Mr Sparks looked in with a grin, which did not improve the expression of his countenance.

"I say, I wouldn't finish that dress to-night if I was you."

"Why not, Phil?" asked the girl in surprise.

"'Cause the lady won't want it to-morrow arternoon."

"How do you know that?"

"No matter. It's by means of a kind of second-sight I've got, that I find out a-many things. All I can say is that I've got a strong suspicion—a what d'ye call it—a presentiment that Mrs Middleton, of Number 6, Conway Street, Knightsbridge, won't want her dress to-morrow, so I advise you to go to bed tonight."

Without waiting for a reply Mr Sparks shut the door and descended to the street. Purchasing and lighting a cheroot at the nearest tobacco shop with part of Martha's last shilling, he thrust his hands into his pockets, and sauntering along various small streets and squares, gave his undivided attention to business.

For a man whose wants were rather extensive and urgent, the "business" did not seem a very promising one. He glanced up at the houses as he sauntered along, appearing almost to expect that some of them would undergo spontaneous combustion for his special accommodation. Occasionally he paused and gazed at a particular house with rapt intensity, as if he hoped the light which flashed from his own eyes would set it on fire; but the houses being all regular bricks refused to flare up at such a weak insult.

Finding his way to Trafalgar Square, Mr Sparks threw away the end of his cheroot, and, mending his pace, walked smartly along Piccadilly until he gained the neighbourhood of Knightsbridge. Here he purchased another cheroot, and while lighting it took occasion to ask if there was a street thereabouts named Conway Street.

"Yes, sir, there is," said a small and exceedingly pert crossing-sweeper, who chanced to be standing near the open door of the shop, and overheard the question. "I'll show you the way for a copper, sir, but silver preferred, if you're so disposed."

"Whereabouts is it?" asked Mr Sparks of the shopman, regardless of the boy.

"Round the corner to your right, and after that second turning to your left."

"Oh, that's all wrong," cried the boy. "W'y, 'ow should 'ee know hanythink about streets? Never goes nowheres, does nothink but sell snuff an' pigtail, mornin', noon, and night. 'Ee should have said, *right* round the corner to your right, and 'ee should have added 'sir,' for that's right w'en a gen'l'm'n's spoke to, arter w'ich, w'en you've left this 'ere street, take second turnin' to your left, if you're left-'anded, an' then you come hall right. That's 'ow 'ee ought to have said it, sir."

In the midst of this flow of information, Mr Sparks emerged into the street.

"I'll show you the way for love, sir, if you ain't got no money," said the boy in a tone of mock sincerity, stepping up and touching his cap.

"Let 'im alone, Bloater," cried another and smaller boy, "don't you see ee's one of the swell mob, an' don't want to 'ave too much attention drawed to him?"

"No 'ee ain't, Little Jim, ee's only a gen'l'm'n in disguise," replied the Bloater, sidling up to Mr Sparks, and urgently repeating, "show you the way for a copper, sir, *only* a copper."

Mr Sparks, being, as we have said, an irascible man, and particularly out of humour that evening, did not vouchsafe a reply, but, turning suddenly round, gave the Bloater a savage kick that turned him head over heels into the road.

The Bloater, whose proper name was Robert Herring, from which were derived the aliases, Raw Herring and the Bloater, immediately recovered himself and rushed at Mr Sparks with his broom. He was a strong, resolute, passionate boy, yet withal good-humoured and placable. In the first burst of indignation he certainly meant to commit a violent assault, but he suddenly changed his mind. Perhaps the look and attitude of his antagonist had something to do with the change; perhaps the squeaky voice of Little Jim, shouting "hooray, Bloater, go in an' win," may have aroused his sense of the ludicrous, which was very strong, and helped to check him. At all events, instead of bringing his broom down on the head of Mr Sparks, Bloater performed an impromptu war-dance round him and flourished his weapon with a rapidity that was only surpassed by the rapid flow of his language.

"Now then, Gunpowder, come on; wot do you mean by it—eh? You low-minded son of a pepper-castor! Who let you out o' the cruet-stand? Wot d'ee mean by raisin' yer dirty foot ag'in a *honest* man, w'ch *you* ain't, an' never was, an' never will be, an' never *could* be, seein' that both your respected parients was 'anged afore you was born. Come on, I say. You ain't a coward, air you? If so, I'll 'and you over to Little Jim 'ere, an' stand by to see fair play!"

During this outburst, Mr Sparks had quietly faced the excited boy, watching his opportunity to make a dash at him, but the appearance of a policeman put a sudden termination to the riot by inducing the Bloater and Little Jim to shoulder their brooms and fly. Mr Sparks, smiling grimly, (he never smiled otherwise), thrust his hands into his pockets, resumed his cheroot, and held on the even tenor of his way.

But he had not yet done with the Bloater. That volatile and revengeful youth, having run on in advance, ensconced himself behind a projection at the corner of the street close to which Sparks had to pass, and from that point of vantage suddenly shot into his ear a yell so excruciating that it caused the man to start and stagger off the pavement; before he could recover himself, his tormentor had doubled round the corner and vanished.

Growling savagely, he continued his walk. One of the turns to the left, which he had to make, led him through a dark and narrow street. Here, keeping carefully in the middle of the road for security, he looked sharply on either side, having his hands out of his pockets now, and clenched, for he fully expected another yell. He was wrong, however, in his expectations. The Bloater happened to know of a long ladder, whose nightly place of repose was on the ground in a certain dark passage, with its end pointing across that street. Taking up a position beside this ladder, with Little Jim—who followed him, almost bursting with delight—he bided his time and kept as quiet as a mouse. Just in the nick of time the ladder was run out, and Mr Sparks tripping over it, fell violently to the ground. He sprang up and gave chase, of course, but he might as well have followed a will-o'-the-wisp. The young scamps, doubling like hares, took refuge in a dark recess under a stair with which they were well acquainted, and from that position they watched their enemy. They heard him go growling past; knew, a moment or two later, from the disappointed tone of the growl, that he had found the opening at the other end of the passage; heard him return, growling, and saw him for a moment in the dim light of the entrance as he left the place. Then, swiftly issuing from their retreat, they followed.

"I say, Bloater," whispered Little Jim, "ee's got such an ugly mug that I do b'lieve ee's up to some game or other."

"P'raps 'ee is," returned the Bloater, meditatively; "we'll let 'im alone an' foller 'im up."

The prolonged season of peace that followed, induced Mr Sparks to believe that his tormentors had left him, he therefore dismissed them from his mind, and gave himself entirely to business. Arrived at Conway street, he found that it was one of those semi-genteel streets in the immediate neighbourhood of Kensington Gardens, wherein dwell thriving tradespeople who know themselves to be rising in the world, and unfortunate members of the "upper ten," who know that they have come down in the world, but have not ceased the struggle to keep up appearances. It was a quiet, unfrequented street, in which the hum of the surrounding city sounded like the roar of a distant cataract. Here Mr Sparks checked his pace—stopped—and looked about him with evident caution.

"Ho, ho!" whispered Little Jim.

"We've tracked 'im down," replied the Bloater with a chuckle.

Mr Sparks soon found Number 6. On the door a brass plate revealed "Mrs Middleton."

"Ha! she *must* have it, must she, an' *won't* take no denial," muttered the man between his teeth.

Mr Sparks observed that one of the lower windows was open, which was not to be wondered at, for the weather was rather warm at the time. He also observed that the curtains of the window were made of white flowered muslin, and that they swayed gently in the wind, not far from a couple of candles which stood on a small table. There was no one in the room at the time.

"Strange," muttered Mr Sparks, with a grim smile, "that people *will* leave lights so near muslin curtains!"

Most ordinary people would have thought the candles in question at a sufficiently safe distance from the curtains, but Mr Sparks apparently thought otherwise. He entertained peculiar views about the danger of fire.

From the position which the two boys occupied they could not see the man while he was thus engaged in examining and commenting on Number 6, Conway Street, but they saw him quite well when he crossed the street, (which had only one side to it, a wall occupying the other), and they saw him still better in the course of a few seconds when a bright light suddenly streamed towards him, and illumined his villainous countenance, and they heard as well as saw him, the next instant, when he shouted "*fire—fire!*" and rushed frantically away.

"Hallo!" exclaimed the Bloater, and dashed off at full speed. Little Jim echoed the sentiment and followed.

Robert, alias Raw Herring, was a sharp-witted lad. He understood the case, (partly at least), in a moment, and proceeded to appropriate action. Being intimately acquainted with that part of

London, he took a short cut, overshot Mr Sparks, and was first to give the alarm at the fire-station. When, therefore, Mr Sparks ran in, panting and shouting "fire!" great was his surprise to find the men already roused, and the horses being attached to the engine.

"Where away?" inquired one of the firemen, supposing that Sparks, perhaps, brought information of another fire.

"Number 6, Conway Street," he gasped.

"All right, we've got the noos already. The boys brought it."

The Bloater, with a mouth extending from ear to ear and all his teeth displayed, uttered the single word "sold!" as Mr Sparks turned his eyes on him. One glance was enough. The man became very pale, and suddenly left the station amid a shout of laughter from the firemen, as they leaped on the engine and drove away, followed by the two boys whose spirits were already excited to the highest pitch of ecstasy by a fire.

It was early morning before the fire was subdued, and Number 6 left the blackened skeleton of a house. Long before that, the Bloater and Little Jim had sought repose in the cart-shed of a neighbouring stable. Long before that Mr Philip Sparks had retired to rest, growling anathemas on the heads of boys in general, and crossing-sweepers in particular; and not *very* long before that poor Martha Reading had put in the last stitch of her work, and fallen into a profound sleep in her chair.

Mr Sparks turned out to be a true prophet. Mrs Middleton did *not* insist on having her dress home that afternoon, and when Martha, true to her promise, conveyed it to Number 6, Conway Street, she found no one there to receive it except a few drenched men of the Red Brigade, and the police.

Chapter Five.

Mr Philip Sparks, though not naturally fond of society, was, nevertheless, obliged to mingle occasionally with that unpleasant body, for the purpose of recruiting his finances. He would rather have remained at home and enjoyed his pipe and beer in solitude, but that was not possible in the circumstances. Owing, no doubt, to the selfishness of the age in which he lived, people would *not* go and pour money into his pockets, entreat him to accept of the same, and then retire without giving him any farther trouble. On the contrary, even when he went out and took a great deal of trouble to obtain money—much more trouble than he would have had to take, had he been an honest working man—people refused to give it to him, but freely gave him a good deal of gratuitous advice instead, and sometimes threatened the donation of other favours which, in many instances, are said to be more numerous than ha'pence.

Things in general being in this untoward condition, Mr Sparks went out one morning and entered into society. Society did not regard him with a favourable eye, but Sparks was not thin-skinned; he persevered, being determined, come what might, to seek his fortune. Poor fellow, like many a man in this world who deems himself a most unlucky fellow, he had yet to learn the lesson that fortunes must be *wrought* for, not *sought* for, if they are to be found.

Finding society gruffer than usual that morning, and not happening to meet with his or anybody else's fortune in any of the streets through which he passed, he resolved to visit Martha Reading's abode; did so, and found her "not at home." With despairing disgust he then went to visit his sister.

Mrs Crashington was obviously at home, for she opened the door to him, and held up her finger.

"Hallo, Mag!" exclaimed Sparks, a little surprised.

"Hush!" said Mrs Crashington, admitting him, "speak low."

Thus admonished, Mr Sparks asked in a hoarse whisper, "what was up?"

"Ned's had a bad fall, Phil," whispered Mrs Crashington, in a tremulous tone that was so unlike her usual voice as to make Sparks look at her in surprise not unmingled with anxiety.

"You don't mean to say, Mag, that he's a-goin' to—to—knock under?"

"I hope not, Phil, but—the doctor—"

Here the poor woman broke down altogether, and sobbed quietly as she led her brother through the house, and into the little bed-room where the injured fireman lay.

Ned's bruised, burned, and lacerated frame was concealed under a patchwork coverlet. Only his face was visible, but that, although the least injured part of his body, was so deadly pale that even Mr Sparks was solemnised by the supposition that he was in the presence of Death.

"Oh, Ned, Ned!" exclaimed Maggie, unable to repress her grief, "can you—can you ever forgive me?"

She laid her hand on the fireman's broad breast, and passionately kissed his brow.

He opened his eyes, and whispered with difficulty, "Forgive you, Maggie? God for ever bless you." He could say no more, owing to excessive weakness.

"Come, missus, you mustn't disturb him," said David Clazie, emerging from behind the curtains at the foot of the bed. "The doctor's orders was strict—to keep 'im quiet. You'd better go into the other room, an' your brother likewise. Pr'aps you might send 'im to tell Joe Dashwood to be ready."

David Clazie, who was more a man of action than of words, quietly, but firmly, ejected the brother and sister from the little room while he was speaking, and, having shut the door, sat down at his post again as a guard over his sick comrade.

"Seems to me it's all up with 'im," observed Sparks, as he stood gazing uneasily into the fire.

As Mrs Crashington replied only by sobbing, he continued, after a few minutes—

"Does the doctor say it's all up, Mag?"

"No, oh no," replied the poor woman, "he don't quite say so; but I can't git no comfort from that. Ned has lost *such* a quantity of blood, it seems impossible for him to git round. They're goin' to try a operation on 'im to-day, but I can't understand it, an' don't believe in it. They talk of puttin' noo blood into 'im! An' that reminds me that the doctor is to be here at twelve. Do run round, Phil, to the Dashwoods, and tell Joe to be here in good time."

"What's Joe wanted for?"

"Never mind, but go and tell him that. I can't talk just now," she said, pushing her brother out of the room.

Tapping at Joe Dashwood's door, Phil received from a strong, deep voice permission to "come in." He entered, and found a very different state of things from that which he had just left. A bright room, and bright, happy faces. The windows were bright, which made the light appear brighter than usual; the grate was bright; the furniture was bright; the face of the clock, whose interior seemed about to explode on every occasion of striking the hour, was bright—almost to smiling; and the pot-lids, dish-covers, etcetera, were bright—so bright as to be absolutely brilliant. Joe Dashwood and his little wife were conversing near the window, but, although their faces were unquestionably bright by reason of contentment, coupled with a free use of soap and the jack-towel, there was, nevertheless, a shade of sadness in their looks and tones. Nothing of the sort, however, appeared on the countenances of the Rosebud and young Fred Crashington. These gushing little offshoots of the Red Brigade were too young to realise the danger of Ned's condition, but they were quite old enough to create an imaginary fire in the cupboard, which they were wildly endeavouring to extinguish with a poker for a "branch" and a bucket for a fire-engine, when Mr Sparks entered.

"Oh! kik, Feddy, kik; put it out kik, or it'll bu'n down all 'e house," cried little May, eagerly, as she tossed back a cataract of golden curls from her flushed countenance, and worked away at the handle of the bucket with all her might.

"All right!" shouted Fred, who had been sent to play with the Rosebud that he might be out of the way. "Down with Number 1; that's your sort; keep 'er goin'; hooray!"

He brought the poker down with an awful whack on the cupboard at this point, causing the crockery to rattle again.

"Hallo! youngster, mind what you're about," cried Joe, "else there will be more damage caused by the engine than the fire—not an uncommon thing, either, in our practice!"

It was at this point that he replied to Mr Sparks's knock.

"Come in, Mr Sparks, you've heard of your poor brother-in-law's accident, I suppose?"

"Yes, I've just comed from his house with a message. You're wanted to be there in good time."

"All right, I'll be up to time," said Joe, putting on his coat and cap, and smiling to his wife, as he added, "It's a queer sort o' thing to do. We'll be blood-relations, Ned and I, after this. Look after these youngsters, Molly, else they'll knock your crockery to bits. Good-day. Mr Sparks."

"Good-day," replied Sparks, as Joe went out. Then, turning to Mrs Dashwood, "What sort of operation is it they're goin' to perform on Ned?"

"Did you not hear? It's a very curious one. Ned has lost so much blood from a deep cut in his leg that the doctors say he can't recover, no matter how strong his constitution is, unless he gits some blood put into him, so they're goin' to put some o' my Joe's blood into him."

"What!" exclaimed Sparks, "take blood out o' your husband and put it hot and livin' into Ned? No, no, I've got a pretty big swallow, but I can't git *that* down."

"If you can't swallow it you'll have to bolt it, then, for it's a fact," returned Mary, with a laugh.

"But how do they mean to go about it?" asked Sparks, with an unbelieving expression of countenance.

"Well, I ain't quite sure about that," replied Mary; "they say that the doctor cuts a hole in a vein of the arms of both men, and puts a pipe, or something of that sort, into the two veins, and so lets the blood run from the one man into the other. I don't half believe it myself, to say truth; but it's quite true that they're goin' to try it on Ned. The doctor says it has bin tried before with great success, and that the main thing is to get a stout, healthy young man to take the blood from. They thought, at first, to get a healthy youth from the country, but my Joe begged so hard to let him supply his friend and comrade with what they wanted, that they agreed, and now he's off to have it done. Ain't it funny?"

"Funny!" exclaimed Sparks, "well, it is, just. But I'm not such a fool as to believe that they can pump the blood out o' one man into another in that fashion."

"I hope they can for poor Ned's sake," said Mary, in a sad tone, as she stirred a large pot which stood simmering on the fire.

There was a short silence after that, for Mary was thinking of the strange operation that was probably going on at that moment, and Phil Sparks was debating with himself as to the propriety of attempting to induce Mrs Dashwood to lend him a shilling or two. He could not easily make up his mind, however; not because he was ashamed to ask it, but, because he was afraid of receiving a rebuke from the pretty little woman. He knew that she and Martha Reading were intimate friends, and he had a suspicion that Mrs Dashwood was aware of Martha's fondness for him, and that she bore him no good will in consequence. Besides, although one of the sweetest tempered women in London, Mary was one whose indignation could be roused, and whose clear blue eye had something overawing in it, especially to scoundrels. He therefore sat there more than an hour, conversing on various subjects, while Mary busied herself in household matters; which she occasionally left off in order to assist in extinguishing the fire in the cupboard!

At last Sparks resolved to make the attempt, and thought he would begin by trying to propitiate Mary by commenting on her child.

"That's a pretty little girl of yours, missis," he remarked in a casual way.

"That she is," cried Mary, catching up the child and kissing her rosy face all over; "and she's better than pretty—she's good, good as gold."

"Oh 'top, ma. Let May down, kik!

Fire not out yit!"

"That's right, never give in, May. Wot a jolly fireman you'd make!" cried Fred, still directing all his energies to the cupboard.

"That's a queer sort o' helmet the boy's got on," said Sparks, alluding to a huge leathern headpiece, of a curious old-fashioned form, which was rolling about on the boy's head, being much too large for him.

"It was bought for him by my Joe, in an old curiosity shop," said Mary.

"Ha!" replied Sparks. "Well, Missis Dashwood, I'll have to be goin', though I haven't got no business to attend to— still, a man must keep movin' about, you know, specially w'en he's had no breakfast, an' han't got nothin' to buy one."

"That's a sad condition," said Mary, pursing her lips, for she knew the man.

"It is, missis. You couldn't lend me half-a-crown, could you?"

"No, I couldn't," replied the little woman with decision, while her cheeks reddened; "moreover, I wouldn't if I could. You ought to be ashamed of yourself, Mr Sparks; it's a disgrace for a man of your strength and years to be goin' about borrowing as you're in the habit of doin'; and you have got the impudence, too, to be running after poor Martha Reading, but you shall never get her if I can prevent it."

Mr Sparks was much nettled by the first part of Mrs Dashwood's speech. The last part put him in a towering passion. He started up, but had the wisdom to restrain himself to some extent.

"Perhaps," he said, between his teeth, "you *can't* prevent it, missis."

"Perhaps not, but I shall try."

At that moment, Master Fred Crashington chanced to stumble in his energetic attempts to extinguish the fire in the cupboard, which the Rosebud assured him, in excited tones, was "not out yit; gittin' wus an' wus!" In falling, the old-fashioned helmet flew off, and the comb of it hit Mr Sparks a severe blow on the shin-bone. In the heat of the moment he dealt Fred a violent slap on the cheek, which sent him tumbling and howling on the floor. At that moment the door opened and Joe Dashwood entered.

He had heard the noise before entering, and now stood with a stern frown on his face as he gazed at his wife and her visitor.

"Did *you* do that?" he demanded of Sparks, pointing to the little boy.

"He did, Joe," said Mary; "but—"

Joe waited for no more. He seized Mr Sparks by the nape of the neck with a grip that almost choked him—strong though he was—and thrust him out of the room, down the stairs, and out into the street, where he gave him a final kick, and shut the door.

"Oh, dear Joe!" exclaimed Mary, on his return, "you shouldn't have been so violent to 'im."

"W'y not, Molly? Surely you would not have me stand by and look on while he insulted you and knocked down the boy?"

"No, but it would have been a better rebuke if you had ordered him off quietly. No good ever comes of violence, Joe, and he's such a spiteful, vindictive man that he will never forgive you— perhaps he'll do you a mischief if he ever gets the chance."

"I hope he will never get the chance," replied Joe. "I hope not, but I fear him," said Mary. "But tell me, Joe, how has the operation succeeded?"

"First-rate, Molly. Ned and I are blood-relations now! I don't know how much they took out o' me, but it don't signify, for I am none the worse, an' poor Ned seems much the better."

Here Joe entered into a minute detail of all that had been done—how a puncture had been made in one of the veins of his arm, and another in one of the veins of Ned's arm; and how the end of a small tube with a bulb in the middle of it had been inserted into *his* puncture, and the other end into *Ned's* puncture, and the blood pumped, as it were, from the full-blooded man into the injured man until it was supposed that he had had enough of it; and how Ned had already shown signs of revival while he, (Joe), didn't feel the loss at all, as was made abundantly evident by the energetic manner in which he had kicked Mr Sparks out of his house after the operation was over.

To all this Mary listened with wide open eyes, and Fred Crashington listened with wider open eyes; and little Rosebud listened with eyes and mouth equally open—not that she understood anything of it, but because the others were in that condition.

"Now, May, my pet," cried the fireman, catching up his little one and tossing her in the air, "Ned, that is so fond of you, is a blood-relation, so you may call him 'uncle' next time he comes— uncle Ned!"

"Unkil Ned," lisped the Rosebud.

"And me cousin," chimed in Fred.

"Iss—cuzn," responded May.

"Just so," cried Joe, seizing Fred round the waist and tossing him on his right shoulder—Rosebud being already on his left—"come, I'll carry you down the fire-escape now; hurrah! down we go."

How long Joe would have gone on playing with the children we cannot say, for he was interrupted by the entrance of Bob and David Clazie.

"Come along, Joe," said the latter, "it's your turn to go along with us to drill."

"It's 'ard work to 'ave to go playin' at fires doorin' the day, an' puttin' of 'em out doorin' the night, Joe; ain't it?" said Bob Clazie.

"So 'tis Bob, but it must be done, you know. Duty first, pleasure afterwards," replied Joe, with a laugh. "Besides, the green hands could never learn how to do it if they hadn't some of the old uns to show 'em the way."

"Hall right," replied Bob; "come along."

They left the room with a hearty "good-day" to Mrs Dashwood, and a nod to the children.

Putting on the round sailor's caps which replaced the helmets when they were not on actual service, the three firemen took their way towards the city, and finally reached a large piece of open ground, where a number of very old houses had been partly pulled down, to be soon replaced by new ones. The Fire-Brigade had obtained permission to perform their drill there until the ground should be required.

It was a curious waste place in the heart of the great city, with rubbish cumbering the ground in front of the half demolished houses. Here several ungainly fire-escapes leaned against the ruined walls, and thrust their heads through broken windows, or stood on the ground, rampant, as if eager to have their heads crammed into smoke and flames. Here also were several manual engines, with their appropriate gearing and hose, and near to these were grouped a band of as fine, fresh, muscular young fellows as one could wish to see. These were the new hands of the brigade—the young men, recently engaged, who were undergoing drill. Each was a picked, and, to some extent, a proved man. The lightest and least powerful among these men was a sturdy, courageous fellow. He, like the others, had been tried at an old fire-escape which stood in a corner of the yard, and which was unusually large and cumbrous. If he had failed to "work" various portions of that escape single-handed, without assistance, he would have been pronounced physically unfit for the service. Courage and strength alone would not have been sufficient. Weight, to a certain extent, was essential.

Among these youths were several of the older hands, and one or two officers of the brigade, the latter being distinguished by brass ornaments or "brasses" on their shoulders. They were there to superintend and direct. In the midst of them stood their chief, explaining the minutiae of the work they had to do.

When our three firemen reached the drill-ground the chief was showing his recruits how to coil several lengths of the hose, so as to avoid a twist or "kink," which might endanger its bursting when the water was turned suddenly on by the powerful "steamers." He then pointed to the tall empty buildings beside him and ordered his recruits to go into the third floor of the premises, drag up the hose, and bring the branch to bear on the back rooms, in which fire was supposed to be raging.

"Look alive, now," he said, "see how quickly you'll manage it."

Instantly the active youths sprang to their work. Some got the hose out of the box of an engine and uncoiled it length by length towards the house, others screwed the lengths together at the same time that the water-trough was being set up and the suction-pipe attached. Meanwhile, some had run up into the building, and from an upper window let down a rope so as to be ready to drag up the hose when it was made long enough to reach them. Thus they practised during the forenoon the mimic warfare with the flames which they should have to carry into actual operation at night. In another part of the yard a foreman was instructing some recruits in the use of the fire-escape. Under a neighbouring archway stood a small group of idlers looking on at these stirring operations, one of these was Philip Sparks, another was the Bloater. The interests of the first had taken him there, the second had been led to the scene by his affections. Sparks did not observe the Bloater, but the Bloater being unusually sharp, had observed Sparks, and, with a look of surprise and glee at the unexpected sight, set himself to watch and listen.

"That's him," growled Sparks in a low whisper, pointing to Joe Dashwood as he entered the yard.

This was said to a dark-skinned, ill-looking, powerful man who stood at his elbow. The man nodded in reply.

"Take a good look at him, Jeff; you'll know him again?"

Jeff nodded and guessed that he would.

"Well, then, West-End; Friday, at 12 p.m. Number 5, close to the fire-station. You won't forget?" whispered Sparks, as he and his ill-looking friend slunk away.

"I say," observed the Bloater, poking Little Jim in the ribs, and looking down at him with one eye shut, "you and I shall form an engagement for Friday night—shan't we."

Little Jim opened his eyes very wide, pressed his mouth very tight, and nodded his head violently.

"Well then," continued the Bloater, repeating Sparks's words in a deep stage whisper, "West-End; Friday, at 12 p.m. Number 5, close to the fire-station. You won't forget?"

Little Jim again nodded his head, and uttered a little shriek of delight. This attracted the notice of a policeman, who hinted, as delicately as possible, that the boys had better "move on."

They took the hint, and retired precipitately.

Chapter Six.

Oh! but it *was* an interesting occupation to watch the expression of Little Jim's countenance, as the Bloater watched it, while the two boys were on their way to the "West-End" that evening, bent on doing duty as amateur watchmen on "Number 5," close to the fire-station.

"Your face ain't cherubic," observed the Bloater, looking down at his little friend. "If anythink, I should say it partakes of the diabolic; so you've got no occasion to make it wus than it is by twistin' it about like that. Wotever do you do it for?"

Little Jim replied by a sound which can only be represented by the letters "sk," pronounced in the summit of the nose.

"That ain't no answer," said the Bloater, with a knowing smile, the knowingness of which consisted chiefly in the corners of the mouth being turned down instead of up. This peculiarity, be it carefully observed, was natural to the Bloater, who scorned every species of affectation. Many of his young friends and admirers were wont to imitate this smile. If they could have seen the inconceivably idiotic expressions of their countenances when they tried it, they would never have made a second effort!

"Wot a jolly lark!" said Little Jim, prefacing the remark with another "sk."

"Ha!" replied the Bloater, with a frown that implied the pressure of weighty matters on his mind.

After a few minutes' silence, during which the cherubic face of Little Jim underwent various contortions, the Bloater said—

"If I ain't mistaken, Jim, you and I are sound of wind and limb?"

Jim looked up in surprise, and nodded assent.

"Besides which," continued the Bloater, "we're rayther fleet than otherwise."

Again Jim nodded and grinned.

"No Bobby as ever stuck 'is hignorant hinsolent 'ead into a 'elmet ever could catch us."

"Sk!" ejaculated Jim, expanding from ear to ear.

"Well, then," continued the Bloater, becoming more grave and confidential, "it's my opinion, Jim, that you and I shall 'ave a run for it to-night. It's quite plain that our hamiable friend who seems so fond o' fire-raisin' is goin' to pay 'is respects to Number 5. 'Avin' got it well alight it is just within the bounds o' the possible—not to say prob'ble—that 'e'll give 'em leg-bail—make tracks, as the Yankees say—cut and run for it. Well, in course it would never do to let 'im go off alone, or with only a 'eavy stoopid, conceited slow-coach of a Bobby at 'is tail."

"No, no," responded Little Jim; "that would never do. Quite out of the question. 'Ighly himproper."

"Therefore," said the Bloater, with emphasis, "you and I shall 'ave to keep our heyes on 'im, shan't we?"

He put this concluding question with a wink of such astounding significance, that Little Jim could only reply with another "sk!" as he stopped for a few moments to hug himself.

At the fire-station "close to Number 5," the firemen lounged about that evening with the air of men who, although they chanced to be idle at the moment, were nevertheless on the alert and ready for action at a moment's notice. Their large folding-doors stood open with an air of off-hand hospitality. A couple of engines stood within, glittering from excessive polish and cleanliness. Coils of hose and buckets, etcetera, were seen here and there in readiness, while in an interior room a glimpse might be had of gleaming brass helmets, which hung in a row on the wall, each with an axe pendant below it; and, opposite to these, a row of dry boots arranged on pegs with their soles to the ceiling.

The two boys lingered about the station admiring all this, and commenting in their own peculiar fashion on men and things, sometimes approvingly, often critically, and now and then disparagingly. They sometimes ventured to address a remark or two to any of the men who chanced to look at them with a sufficiently good-humoured expression, and even went the length of asking Bob Clazie if, in the event of the Thames going on fire, "'e thought 'e could manage to put it hout!" to which Bob replied that he thought he could if "cheek" were a fire-extinguisher, and he only had a brigade of boys equal to the Bloater to help him.

As the night advanced the firemen devoted themselves to pipes, draughts, and miscellaneous conversation in their back room, in which they were occasionally interrupted by the tingle of the telegraphic bell, to inform them that there was a chimney on fire in Holborn, to which they need pay no attention, even though "called" by an excited informer, because it was already being attended to, and didn't merit farther notice; or to let them know that there was a fire raging in Whitechapel, which, although being most energetically looked after by the men of the brigade in its immediate neighbourhood, would be the better of aid, nevertheless, from *one* man from that station.

On such distant duty, Bob Clazie and his brother David were successively sent out in different directions during the first part of the night; but they returned in the course of an hour or so—Bob considerably dirtied and moistened in consequence of having had to go vigorously into action at the tail end of a fire, while David returned as he went, having found that *his* fire had been effectually got under before his arrival.

Only once during the night did a regular "call" reach the station. It was about eleven o'clock. Our youthful watchmen, feeling that the appointed hour was drawing nigh, had retired to the shade of a neighbouring court to avoid observation, when a man came tearing round the corner, dashed into the fire-station, tumbled over a bucket into the midst of the men, and yelled, "Fire!"

In three minutes the engine was out, the horses were attached, the men in their places, and away they went.

"Oh! let's follow," cried Little Jim, enthusiastically, while his eyes glittered as if they, too, were on fire.

The more sedate Bloater laid his hand heavily on his little friend's shoulder.

"No, Jim, no. Business fust, pleasure arterwards. We've got business on hand to-night."

Little Jim felt the force of the observation, and made what we may call a mighty effort—considering that he was such a mite of a thing—to restrain himself. His heroism was rewarded, for, in less than half an hour, the engine came rattling back again, its services not having been required! The fire had occurred close to the fire-escape, of which one of the men of that station had the charge that night. He had run to the fire with his escape at the first alarm, and had brought to bear on it the little hand fire-engine with which all the escapes are now provided. At that early stage in the fire, its little stream was more effectual than the flood from a powerful "steamer" would have been at a later period. The consequence was that the fire was got under at once, and, as we have said, the engine was not required.

"Wirtoo," observed the Bloater, sententiously, "is its own reward."

He pointed to the returning engine, and looked at Little Jim with solemnity; whereupon Jim displayed all his teeth, nodded approval of the sentiment, and—"sk!"

"Little Jim," continued the Bloater, shaking his head gravely, "they do say—them as knows best, or thinks they does, which is all the same—that there's wit in silence; if so, it appears to me that you tries to be too witty at times."

"I dun know, Bob," replied Jim, with a meditative look, "much about wit bein' in silence. I only wish there was wittles in it. Oh! wouldn't I 'old my tongue, just, till I was fit to bust!"

"But there ain't wittles in it, Jim, nor nothin' else worth 'avin', so don't try it on too much to-night. You see, I'm a bit down-'earted about the thoughts o' this 'ere black business, an' feel the want of a cheerin' word now and agin to keep up my droopin' spirits, d'ye see; so don't stand grinnin' there like a Cheshire cat, else I'll—"

The Bloater terminated the sentence in action, by squeezing Little Jim's cap over his eyes. He was still engaged in this act of pleasantry when Mr Sparks and his friend Jeff appeared on the other side of the street. They walked smartly past the door of the fire-station, which was shut by that time, the men having retired to their various domiciles for the night, with the exception of the two on night duty. They stopped at the corner of the street, looked back, and stood as if conversing casually with each other. Meanwhile, the two boys shrank out of sight, and gazed at them like weasels peeping out of a hole. The street, being a small back one, was quite deserted at that hour. After talking in low tones for a few seconds, and making sure, as Jeff said, that the coast was clear, the incendiaries shrunk round the corner and disappeared.

"Now, Jim," whispered the Bloater, "they've gone to Number 5; let's foller."

They were uncommonly active and sly little fellows, but, despite their utmost efforts, they failed to gain a position of vantage from which to observe the enemy without being seen. They did, indeed, manage to make out that the two men were for some time busily and stealthily engaged in the neighbourhood of Joe Dashwood's dwelling, but what they were doing could not be ascertained. After repeated and desperate efforts to overcome his difficulties, at the risk of his neck and to the detriment of his shins, the Bloater at last sat down on a doorstep within a dark passage, and feigned to tear his hair.

"Now ain't it wexin'?" he whispered, appealing to his small friend.

"Aggravatin' beyond endoorance," replied Jim, with looks of sympathy.

"Wot *is* to be done?" demanded the Bloater.

"Invite a Bobby to come an' help us," suggested Jim.

"H'm! an' stop 'em in their game, p'raps, at a pint w'ere nobody could prove nothink against 'em, besides bringin' on ourselves the purlite inquiry, 'Wot are *you* up to 'ere?'"

Little Jim looked disconsolate and said nothing, which, as the Bloater testily remarked, was another of his witty rejoinders.

"Well, then," said Jim, "we must just wait till the fire breaks out an' then bust upon 'em all of a 'eap."

"H'm! much they'd care for *your* bustin' on 'em. No, Jim, we must risk a little. Never wenter, never win, you know. Just you go round by the other end of the street and creep as close as you can; you're small, you know, an' won't be so easy seen as me. Try to make out wot they're up to and then—"

"Then wot?"

"W'y, come back an' let me know. Away!" said the Bloater, waving his hand with the air of a field-marshal.

Jim disappeared at once and was absent about ten minutes, during which Master Robert Herring sat in the dark passage biting his nails and feeling really uncomfortable, as is usually the case with energetic spirits when reduced to unavoidable inaction. Presently Little Jim returned with, as his friend and patron remarked, his eyes like two saucers, and his face as white as a sheet.

"Hallo, Jim, wot's up?"

"Oh, Bob!" gasped Jim.

"Speak!" exclaimed the Bloater, seizing him by the shoulders and shaking him violently.

"They've got the 'ouse choke full o' combustibles," gasped Jim in an excited whisper. "I see 'em stuffin' straw and pitch, an' I dun know wot all, through a small back winder."

"So—*now's* the time for a Bobby," observed the Bloater, leaping up.

"No, taint," said Jim, detaining him. "I 'eard 'em speak. Oh, they're sly dogs! They ain't a-goin' to run away arter settin' it alight. They're goin' to run to the station, rouse up the men, an' help to put it out! an' one of 'em says, 'Jeff,' says 'e, larfin', 'won't we lend 'em a good 'and to put it hout neither!' And the other grinned, an' says, 'Yes, Phil, we'll do our best, an' it'll go hard if I can't in the middle o' the smoke an' flames, git a chance at Joe to—.' 'E didn't say no more, but 'e drewed 'is finger across 'is throat; but the one as 'e called Phil said, 'No, Jeff, no, I'll split on you if you do. It's quite enough to give 'im a rap over the 'ead!' I didn't wait to 'ear no more arter that."

"They're safe not to go off, then," observed the Bloater; "nevertheless, we must take a Bobby into our confidence now, for the case begins to look ugly."

While these things were transpiring in the dark and silent night outside of "Number 5," the inmates of that modest mansion were buried in profound repose. Joe Dashwood, on leaving the station for the night, and going home, had found that Molly had already retired, and was asleep in the inner room with the Rosebud in her bosom.

After contemplating this pleasant sight for a few minutes he returned to the outer or kitchen-dino-drawing-room, where he found a cot extemporised out of four chairs and a baking-board, on which reposed the sturdy little figure of Fred Crashington. That enthusiastic amateur fireman had been invited to take up his quarters at Number 5, until his father should be out of danger, and having devoted his energies during the entire day, along with the Rosebud, in a futile effort to extinguish that obstinate fire in the cupboard, had at length been persuaded to retire exhausted to the baking-board, where he lay with a happy smile on his parted lips, and his right arm embracing the quaint old helmet, with which he was wont to extinguish his little head.

Being unusually tired that night, but not sleepy, Joe resolved to solace himself with a pipe before lying down. He threw off his coat, vest, and braces, pulled up his flannel shirt, so as to let it hang comfortably loose over the waistband of his trousers, sat down in an armchair in front of the fire, filled his pipe, and began to smoke. His intention was to "take a few whiffs and then turn in," but the influence of the tobacco appeared to be soporific, for he soon began to nod; then he removed his pipe, stared earnestly at the fire, and established quite a nodding acquaintance with it. Presently he dropped his chin on his broad chest and snored steadily.

From this condition of repose he was awakened by a sensation as if of suffocation by smoke. This was such an extremely natural, not to say habitual, state of things with Joe, that he was at least a couple of seconds in realising the fact that there was unusual cause for haste and vigorous action. Like a giant refreshed Joe leaped to his work. Every fibre of his huge frame was replete with energy, and his heart beat strong, but it beat steadily; not a vestige of a *flutter* was there, for his head was clear and cool. He knew exactly what to do. He knew exactly what was being done. Surprise did, indeed, fill him when he *reflected* that it was his own house which had caught fire, but that did not for a moment confuse him as to the certainty that the engine must be already out, and his comrades rushing to his assistance.

He strode to the door and opened it. A volume of dense black smoke, followed by sheets of flame drove him back. At the same moment loud shouts were heard outside, and a shriek came from the inner room. Joe dashed towards it. In passing, he pulled Fred off the baking-board, and at the same moment seized the curious old helmet, and almost instinctively clapped it on his own head. There was a back door to the house. Joe grasped his wife, and the Rosebud, and the bedclothes in one mighty embrace, and bore the whole bundle towards this back door. Before he reached it it was dashed open by Bob Clazie, who sprang in with the "branch." Bob, having been roused to a fire so near at hand, had not taken time to go through the usual process of putting on his uniform. He, like Joe, was in dishabille.

"Here, take care of 'em. Let go the branch; I'll look after it. Foul play here. Let the police look out."

Joe said this sharply as he thrust the bundle containing his wife into Bob's arms, and, picking up the Rosebud, who had slipped out, clapped her on Bob's back. Bob made for the back staircase, while Joe picked up the branch, and turning his head in the direction of the open door, shouted in the voice of a stentor, "Down with 'er!" Meanwhile, Fred, who had a vague impression that the fire in the cupboard had got to a powerful head at last, picked up the hose and looked on with a sleepy smile.

Obedient to the order, the water rushed on, filled and straightened the hose, threw Fred on his back on the floor, and caused the nozzle to quiver as Joe directed it to the fire.

Just then a man dashed into the room.

"Lend a hand here," cried Joe glancing round.

He saw in a moment by the man's look that he meant mischief. Instantly he turned the nozzle full in his face. Jeff, for it was he, fell as if he had been shot, and was partly washed, partly rolled down the back staircase, at the foot of which a policeman was prepared to receive him, but Jeff sprang up, knocked down the policeman, and fled. Seeing this, Mr Sparks took alarm, and was about to follow when the Bloater suddenly sprang at his throat and Little Jim caught him by the legs. He quickly disengaged himself, however, and ran off at full speed, closely followed by his young tormentors and two policemen, besides a miscellaneous crowd of hooting and yelling lads and boys.

It was an exciting chase that ensued. The two policemen were young and strong, and for some time kept pretty near the fugitive, but gradually they fell behind, and, by doubling through several narrow streets, Sparks threw them off the scent. As for the crowd, the greater part of those who composed it gave in after a short run. But the Bloater and Little Jim were not thus to be got rid of. They were fleet of foot and easily kept Mr Sparks in view, though he made desperate efforts to catch them, as well as to get away from them. The two boys were so persevering that they followed him all the way to Thames Street, and, just when the unhappy man thought he had at length eluded them, they set up the cry of "Stop thief!" and gave chase again with a new force of policemen and roughs at their heels.

Turning abruptly into a dark passage, Sparks rushed upstairs, burst open a door and fell exhausted on the floor of the cheerless room occupied by poor Martha Reading. Almost at the same moment the two boys, who were at least a hundred yards in advance of the other pursuers, sprang into the room.

"Ha! run you down at last, have we?" gasped the Bloater.

Poor startled Martha, leaping at once to the conclusion that he was pursued, fell on her knees, and, in a voice of agonising entreaty, begged the boys to have mercy on him!

"Eh! hallo! what?" exclaimed the Bloater, taken by surprise. Then, under a sudden impulse, he dashed out of the room followed by Little Jim, and rushed into the street just as the first of the crowd came up.

"This way! Straight on! hooray!" he shouted, leading off the crowd in the direction of the river. The crowd followed. The Bloater led them into a maze of intricate back streets; shot far ahead of them, and then, doubling, like a hare, into a retired corner, stood chuckling there while the shouting crowd swept by.

For a few minutes, Little Jim was utterly bereft of speech, owing to a compound of amazement, delight, excitement and exhaustion. After a little time he said—

"Well, this *is* a lark! But, I say, Bloater, d'ye think it was right to let 'im off like that?"

"Who's let 'im off, stoopid?" retorted the Bloater.

"Don't I know 'is name—at least part of it; an' the 'abitation of 'is wife, or sweet-'eart, or sister, or suthin' o' that sort?"

"Oh, ah, werry true," replied Little Jim, with a terminating "sk!"

"Well, that bein' 'ow it is, we han't let 'im off just yet, d'ye see? So, now we'll go an' turn in."

With that observation the Bloater and Little Jim went away to search for and appropriate some convenient place of repose for the night.

Chapter Seven.

Seated by the fire-side of Joe Dashwood's new abode—for the old one, although not quite "burnt out," was uninhabitable—Bob Clazie chatted and smoked his pipe contentedly. At the conclusion of a remark, he looked up in Mrs Dashwood's puzzled face, and said, "That's 'ow it is, d'ye see?"

"No, I don't see," replied Mary, with a smile.

"No? well, now, that *is* koorious. W'y, it's as plain as the nose on my face. See here. As the law now stands, there is no public authority to inwestigate the cause o' fires in London; well, wot's the consikence, w'y, that there are regular gangs of scoundrels who make it their business to arrange fires for their own adwantage."

"Now, that's just what I don't understand," said Mary, knitting her pretty brows; "what advantage *can* it be to any one to set fire to a house, except to pickpockets who may get a chance of doing business in the crowd?"

"Well, that of itself is enough to endooce some blackguards to raise a fire, and likewise to get the shillin' for bringin' the first noose to the station; which, by the way, was the chief okipation of that willain Phil Sparks, I'm pretty sure. But here's 'ow it is. The swindlers I speak of, go an' take 'ouses—the further from fire-stations the better. Then they furnishes the 'ouses, arter which they insures 'em. In the course of a short time they removes most of the furniture in a quiet way, and then set the 'ouses alight, themselves escapin', p'r'aps, in nothin' but their night clothes. So, you see, they gits the insurance, which more than pays for all the furniture they had bought, besides which they 'ave a good deal of the furniture itself to sell or do wot they please with. That's one way in which fires are raised,—ain't it Joe?"

Joe, who sat smoking in silence on the other side of the fire, nodded, and, turning his head round, advised Fred Crashington and little May to make "less row."

"But we can't put it out widout a row!" remonstrated the Rosebud.

"What! have you found a fire in *this* cupboard, as well as in the one o' the old house?" asked Joe, with a laugh.

"Iss, iss; an' it's a far wuss fire than the last one!"

"That's your sort!" cried Fred; "now then, May, don't stand jawin' there, but down with number two. Look alive!"

"Ha! chips o' the old blocks, I see," said Bob Clazie, with a grin. "Well, as I was sayin', there's another class o' men, not so bad as the first, but bad enough, who are indooced to go in for this crime of fire-raisin'—arson they calls it, but why so is beyond me to diskiver. A needy tradesman, for instance, when at his wits'-end for money, can't help thinkin' that a lucky spark would put him all right."

"But how could the burning of his goods put him all right?" demanded Mary.

"W'y, 'e don't want goods, you know, 'e wants to sell 'is goods an' so git *money*; but nobody will buy, so 'e can't sell, nor git money, yet money must be 'ad, for creditors won't wait. Wot then? All the goods are insured against fire. Well, make a bonfire of 'em, redooce 'em all to hashes, an' of coorse the insurance companies is bound to pay up, so 'e gits rid of the goods, gits a lot o' ready money in 'and, pays off 'is creditors, and p'r'aps starts fresh in a noo business! Now, a public officer to inwestigate such matters would mend things to some extent, though 'e mightn't exactly cure 'em. Some time ago the Yankees, I'm told, appointed a officer they called a fire-marshal in some of their cities, and it's said that the consikence was a sudden an' extraor'nary increase in the conwictions for arson, followed by a remarkable decrease in the number o' fires! They've got some-thin' o' the same sort in France, an' over all the chief towns o' Europe, I b'lieve, but we don't need no such precautions in London. We're rich, you know, an' can afford to let scamps burn right an' left. It ain't worth our while to try to redooce the number of *our* fires. We've already got an average of about five fires every twenty-four hours in London. Why should we try to make 'em less, w'en they furnishes 'ealthy work to such fine fellows as Joe and me and the police—not to mention the fun afforded to crossin'-sweepers and other little boys, whose chief enjoyment in life would be gone if there was no fires."

"If *I* had the making of the laws," exclaimed Mary, flushing with indignation as she thought of her own recent risks and losses in consequence of fire-raising, "I'd have every man that set light to his house *hanged*!"

"Ah; an' if 'e could also be draw'd and quartered," added Bob, "and 'ave the bits stuck on the weathercocks of Saint Paul's, or atop of Temple Bar, it would serve 'im right."

"We must have you into Parliament some day, Molly," said Joe, with a smile. "Women are tryin' hard, I believe, to get the right to vote for members; w'y not go the whole hog and vote themselves in?"

"They'd make splendid firemen too," said Clazie, "at least if they were only half as vigorous as your little May. By the way, Joe," continued Bob, "has Sparks been took yet?"

"Not yet. It is rumoured that the crossin'-sweeper who chased him down so smartly, suddenly favoured his escape at last, from some unaccountable cause or other. I suppose that Sparks bribed him."

"You're sure it was Sparks, are you?" inquired Bob.

"Quite sure. It is true I only saw his confederate, but one of the men who had often seen Sparks in company with Crashington, his brother-in-law, knew him at once and saw him run off, with the boys after him. He's a bad lot, but I hope he'll escape for poor Mrs Crashington's sake."

"And *I* hope he won't escape, for poor Martha Reading's sake!" said Mary with much decision of tone.

"That's his sweet-'eart—a friend of Molly's!" said Joe to Bob in explanation.

At this point in the conversation, Master Fred Crashington, in his frantic efforts to reach an elevated part of the cupboard, fell backwards, drawing a shelf and all its contents on the top of himself and May. Neither of them was hurt, though both were much frightened.

"I think *that* must have put the fire out at last," said Joe, with a laugh, as he took the panting rosebud on his knee and smoothed her soft little head. "We'll sit quiet now and have a chat."

A knock at the outer door here called Mrs Dashwood from the room.

"Fire!" exclaimed May, holding up her finger and listening with eager expectation.

"No, little woman," said Joe, "they would ring loud if it was fire."

Meanwhile Mrs Dashwood opened the door and found herself confronted by a boy, with his hands in his pockets and his cap thrown in a reckless way half on the side and half on the back of his head.

"Oh, I suppose you are the boy Herring, sent here by Miss Reading," said Mrs Dashwood.

"Well, as to that, ma'am, you must be guided by taste. I've 'eard of men of my years an' standin' bein' styled 'obble-de-'oys. My name, likewise, is open to question. Some of my friends calls me 'Erring—others of 'em, Raw 'Erring—others, again, the Bloater. But I'm in no wise partikler, I *did* come from Miss Reading to 'ave an interview with Mrs Dashwood—whom—I presoom—"

Here the Bloater laid his hand on his heart and made a courtly bow.

Mrs Dashwood laughed, and said, "come in, boy."

"I have a pal, ma'am—a chum—a—in fact a *friend*—may I—"

Without finishing his sentence or waiting for a reply, the Bloater gave a sharp whistle, and Little Jim stood by his side as if by magical influence, looking the embodiment of united innocence and impudence.

"Come in, both of you, and make haste," said Mary, ushering them into a small empty room. "Now, boy—"

"Bloater, ma'am, if you 'ave no objection."

"Well, Bloater, our communication with each other must be brief and to the point, because—"

"Yes, ma'am—sharp and short," interrupted the Bloater—"reasons not required."

Smiling in spite of herself, Mrs Dashwood said—

"You know Mr Sparks, and can—can—in short, give him into the hands of justice."

"If I knowed w'ere justice was," said the Bloater, sternly, "p'raps I might give Mr Sparks into 'is 'ands, but I don't. It's my opinion that *justice* ain't finished yet. They've made 'is 'ands no doubt—and pretty strong ones they are too—but they 'aven't give 'im brains yet. 'Ows'ever, to make a long story short, 'as 'Amlet said to 'is father's ghost, w'ich was prince of Timbuctoo, I *do* know Mr Sparks, and I *can* give 'im into the 'ands of the p'lice—wot then?"

"*Do it!*" said Mrs Dashwood, with sudden intensity of feeling and manner, "Do it, boy—" ("Bloater," murmured the lad), "do it, Bloater. Oh! you have no idea what a blessing it would be to—to—to—a poor, dear girl who is mad—infatuated and, and—then, he is *such* a scoundrel; such a fire-raiser, deceiver, villain—"

"You don't appear to like 'im yourself," remarked the Bloater.

He said this so quietly and with an air of calmness which contrasted so strongly with Mrs Dashwood's excitement, that Little Jim gave vent to an irresistible "sk" and blew his nose violently to distract attention from it.

"Will you not consent to give up a thorough scoundrel, who every one condemns?" demanded Mrs Dashwood, with sudden indignation.

"Well, that depends—"

"Bloater," said Mary, with increasing earnestness, "I cannot bribe you—I have not the means even if I had the will; but I would not if I could. I scorn bribery. If you will not aid me for the sake of a poor, helpless, infatuated girl, who is on the brink of ruin—"

"Missis Dashwood," said the Bloater, with a look of serio-comic dignity, "I scorns bribery as much as you does. 'No bribery, no c'rupt'ons, no Popery,' them's my mottoes—besides a few more that there's no occasion to mention. W'ether or not I gives 'im up depends on circumstances. Now, I s'pose *you* want's 'im took an' bagged, 'cause 'e ain't fit for your friend Martha Reading—we'll drop the 'Miss' if you please. Well, wot I want to know is, does Martha think as you does?"

"Of course not, boy. No doubt she knows that he is an unworthy scoundrel, but she can't prevail on herself to forsake him; so, you see, I want to help her a little."

"Ah, I see—yes—I see. Well, missis, I'll take it into consideration. Come along, Jim."

Without waiting for a reply, the Bloater quitted the house abruptly, followed by his friend. He walked very fast towards the City—so fast that Jim was compelled to trot—and was unusually silent. He went straight to the abode of Martha Reading, and found her sewing and weeping.

"Ha! *he's* bin with you, I see," said the Bloater. "Did 'e ask you to let 'im 'ide 'ere?"

"Ye-es;" said Martha, hesitating; "but I refused to do it. God knows how willing—how willing—I would be to shelter and save him if I could!"

"Would you shelter a *guilty* man?" demanded the Bloater, sternly.

"I don't know that he is guilty," said Martha, evasively. "But, tell me, what did Mrs Dashwood want with you?"

"That's a private matter," said the Bloater, frowning. "You can't turn me off the scent like that. I ask you, ain't it right to 'and a guilty man over to justice?"

"It is," replied Martha, wiping her eyes, "but it is also right to temper justice with mercy."

"I say, that's drawin' it rather fine, ain't it?" said the Bloater, screwing up one eyebrow and turning towards Little Jim; but that small youth was so touched with the poor girl's sorrow and so attracted by her countenance, that he had quite forgotten his patron for the moment. Going towards her, he laid his dirty little hand on her knee, and looked up in her face.

"God bless you, dear boy," she said, patting him on the head, "you are the first that has given me a look of sympathy for many—"

She broke down suddenly, burst into a flood of tears, and, seizing the child in her arms, absolutely hugged him!

"Hallo! hallo!" cried the Bloater, when Little Jim was released. "I say, you know, come, this sort o' thing will never do. W'y, its houtrageous. Come along with you."

Saying which he seized Little Jim by the collar, dragged him out into the street, and hurried him along. Presently he released him, but without slackening his pace, and said, "Now, Jim, you an' I shall go and pay *another* wisit."

They traversed several small streets, which seemed to be influenced by a tendency to gravitate towards the Thames; while the river, as if in sympathy, appeared to meet them more than half way in the shape of mud. As they proceeded, huge warehouses frowned above, having doors high up on their blank faces where windows ought to have been, with no steps leading thereto, but in some cases with huge block tackles pendent therefrom, suggestive of the idea that the owners were wont to drop the enormous hooks and fish for passers-by. These streets naturally became more nautical in some respects as they neared the river. Old bits of timber lay here and there among old cordage in little yards, where the owners appeared to deal in small-coal and miscellaneous filth. Elsewhere, worn-out anchors held tenaciously to the mud, as if afraid of being again pressed into service and carried off to sea. Everything was cold, dismal, dreary, disreputable; and here, in the dirtiest corner of the smallest possible yard, the Bloater found a half-concealed door that might have been the portal to a dog-kennel or pig-sty. Opening it he entered, and Little Jim followed.

The aspect of things inside was not attractive. Dirt, damp, and rubbish prevailed in the room, which was just big enough to permit of a tall man lying down, but not high enough to admit of his standing up. An uncommonly small four-post bed almost filled the apartment, at the foot of which, on the floor and half-reclining against one of the posts, lay Phil Sparks, either dead-drunk or asleep, or both.

The Bloater glanced back at Little Jim with a look of satisfaction, and held up his finger to enjoin silence. Peering round the room, which was lighted by a farthing candle stuck in the neck of a pint bottle, he observed a piece of rope lying among some rubbish.

"Ha! this'll do," he whispered, as he took it up, and, with wonderful rapidity, made a loop on it.

"Now, Jim, you be ready to cut and run if he should waken before I 'ave 'im fast. Don't mind me; I'll look arter myself. An' wotever you do, *don't holler for the bobbies*. Mind that, else I'll strangle you."

With this advice and caution, the Bloater advanced toward the recumbent man, and passed the rope softly round his body, including his arms and the bedpost in the coil. Drawing it suddenly tight, he hastily made it fast; but there was no occasion for haste, for the sleep of the man was so profound that the action did not awake him.

"Hall right—fus' rate," said the Bloater aloud, as he wound the rope round and round Sparks, so as to make him doubly secure. "Nothin' could be better. Now, Jim, I'm goin' for to preach a sermon to-night—a sort o' discoorse. You never heard me preach, did you?"

Little Jim, who, despite his love of mischief, was somewhat alarmed at the strange proceedings of his friend and patron, looked at him with a mingled expression of fear and glee, and shook his head.

"Well, you shall 'ear. Moreover, I 'ope that you'll profit by wot you 'ears."

Saying this, he advanced his hand towards the sleeping man's face, and, causing his thumb to act as a trigger to his middle finger, gave him such a flip on the point of his nose, that he awoke with a tremendous roar. Suddenly he became pale as death—supposing, no doubt, that he had betrayed himself—and glanced towards the door with a bewildered stare.

"Oh, you needn't alarm yourself," said the Bloater, placing a stool in front of his victim, and sitting down thereon, with a hand on each knee, "it ain't the bobbies. If you keep quiet, there's no fear of *them* in this neighbourhood. I can call 'em w'en I wants 'em. There's nobody but me and Little Jim 'ere—your friends, you know."

Becoming suddenly convinced of the truth of this, Phil Sparks, who was very drunk, made so desperate an effort to free himself that he nearly overturned the bed.

"Oh, you are anxious to see the bobbies, are you? Well, go an' call 'em in, Jim."

Jim rose to obey, and the man became instantly quiet.

"Ho! you're reasonable now, are you? That's well. You needn't call 'em in yet, Jim. We'll grant 'im a reprieve. Fetch that stool, an' sit down beside me—there. Now, Mr Sparks, *alias* Blazes, no doubt *you're* a precious specimen of hinnocent 'unmanity, ain't you?"

Sparks made no reply, but scowled at the boy with a look of deadly hatred.

"Well, upon my word," resumed the Bloater, with a smile, "if I kep' a menagerie, I'd offer you five 'undred a year to represent a Tasmanian devil. But look 'ere, now, I've no time to waste with you; I come 'ere to give you a bit of my mind. You're a fire-raiser, you are. Ah! you may well wince an' grow w'ite. You'd grow w'iter still, with a rope round your neck, if you wos left to *my* tender mercies, you w'ite livered villain! for I knows you; I've watched you; I've found you hout; an' I've only got to 'old up my little finger to cut your pretty little career prematoorly short. You don't seem to like that? No, I didn't expect you would. This young man, whose 'art is big, if 'is body's small, knows as much about you as I do. Two witnesses, you see; but you *ain't* left to *our* tender mercies; and if you wants to know who delivered you from us, and from the maginstrates, and Jack Ketch, *alias* Calcraft, I replies, *Martha Reading*. Ha! you look surprised. Quite nat'ral. You've deserved very different treatment from that young ooman, an' didn't expect that she'd return good for evil, I s'pose. That's because you don't know 'er; you don't understand 'er, you miserable lump of selfish stoopidity.

'Ows'ever, as I said before, I ain't a-goin' to waste no more time with you. But let me, before biddin' you adoo, give you a caution. Remember, that *I've got my eye on you.* Just one word more. W'en you thinks of *me*, don't think of one as 'as got any tender mercies, for I ain't got none; not a scrap of 'em, nor nothin' of the sort. W'en you wants to know the true cause of your bein' let off, just think of two words—*Martha Reading*! She knows nothin' o' wot I'm doin', nevertheless, *she's* done it! Let 'er name ring in your ears, an' thunder in your brain, and burn in your 'art, till it consooms your witals or your willany! Now, Jim," concluded the Bloater, rising and opening a large clasp-knife, "you go to the door, open it wide, an' stan' by to cut, and run. This gen'lm'n ain't to be trusted w'en free. Are you ready?"

"Hall ready," replied Jim.

The Bloater cut the cord that bound Phil Sparks, and darted from the room. Before the man could disentangle himself from its coils, the boys were safe from pursuit, quietly wending their way through the crowded thoroughfares of the great city.

Chapter Eight.

Several months passed away. During this period Phil Sparks kept in close hiding, because, although the Bloater, true to his promise, refrained from giving information against him, there were others who knew and suspected him, and who had no visions of an imploring Martha to restrain them in their efforts to deliver him into the hands of justice.

During this period, also, Ned Crashington recovered his wonted health and vigour, while his wife, to some extent, recovered her senses, and, instead of acting as an irritant blister on her husband, began really to aim at unanimity. The result was, that Ned's love for her, which had only been smothered a little, burst forth with renewed energy, and Maggie found that in peace there is prosperity. It is not to be supposed that Maggie was cured all at once. She was not an angel—only an energetic and self-willed woman. She therefore broke out now and then in her old style; but, on the whole, she was much improved, and the stalwart fireman no longer sought martyrdom in the flames.

During this period, too, the men of the Red Brigade held on the even tenor of their furious fiery way; not, indeed, scatheless, but with a much smaller amount of damage to life and limb than might have been expected in a service where the numerical strength was so low—only about 380 men—and where the duty, night and day, was so severe and hazardous.

About this time, their Chief's "Report" for the past year was issued, and it revealed a few facts which are worthy of record. It stated that there had been altogether 1946 fires in London during the past twelve months; that is, an average of a little more than five fires every twenty-four hours. Of these 1670 had been slight, while 276 were serious. In these fires 186 persons had been seriously endangered, of whom 153 were rescued by the men of the Red Brigade, while 33 perished, despite the most gallant efforts to save them. The Report showed, further, that there were in London at that time, (and it is much the same still), 50 fire-engine stations, 25 land steam fire-engines, 85 manual fire-engines, 2 floating steam fire-engines on the Thames, and 104 fire-escapes. The number of journeys made by the fire-engines during the year was 8127, and the total distance run was 21,914 miles. This, the reader will observe, implies an enormous amount of labour performed by the 380 heroes who constitute the Red Brigade, and who, although thus heavily overtaxed, were never heard to murmur or complain. That they suffered pretty frequently and severely might have been expected. In truth, it is a marvel that they did not suffer more. The Report showed that, among them all in the course of the year, they had received 36 contusions, dislocations, fractures, and such like injuries; 22 incised, lacerated, and punctured wounds; 18 injuries to eyes, head, and arms; 2 internal injuries; 22 sprains, and, strange to say, only 4 burns and scalds, making 104 injuries altogether, but no deaths.

Things being in this condition, the brigade lay on its oars, so to speak, awaiting "a call," one bleak evening in November, when everything in London looked so wet, and cold, and wretched, that some people went the length of saying that a good rousing fire would be quite a cheering sight for the eyes to rest upon.

In the West-End station, to which we have directed attention more than once in this tale, Joe Dashwood, and Ned Crashington, and Bob Clazie, with his brother David, and some more of the men, were seated in the inner lobby, discussing the news of the day, and settling the affairs of the nation to their own entire satisfaction. The Bloater and Little Jim were also there, hanging about the door. These fire-eating youths had become so fond of the locality and of the men, that they had taken to sweeping a crossing in the neighbourhood, and were wont to cheer their spirits, during intervals of labour, by listening to, or chaffing, the firemen, and following them, when possible, to fires.

Suddenly the rattle of the telegraphic bell roused the men. This was so common an occurrence, that it scarcely called forth a passing remark. One of them, however, rose with alacrity, and, replying to the signal, read off the message. We cannot give the precise words of the telegram, but it was to the effect that a fire had broken out at Saint Katharine's Docks, and that all available force was to be sent out at once.

On hearing this there was unusual promptitude in the movements of the firemen. At all times they are bound, on pain of a heavy fine, to turn out in three minutes after receiving the call to a fire. Sometimes they succeed in turning out in less. It was so on the present occasion. Mention of a fire anywhere near the docks has much the same effect on the Red Brigade as the order to march to the field of Waterloo had on the British army. The extreme danger; the inflammable nature of the goods contained in the huge and densely-packed warehouses; the proximity to the shipping; the probability of a pitched battle with the flames; the awful loss of property, and perhaps of life, if the fire should gain the mastery, and the urgent need there is for hurrying all the disposable force in London to the spot without delay, if the victory is to be gained—all these circumstances and considerations act as an unusually sharp spur to men, who, however, being already willing at all times to do their utmost, can only force themselves to gain a few additional moments of time by their most strenuous exertions.

In less than three minutes, then, our West-End engine sprang off, like a rocket, at full gallop, with a crack of the whip, a snort from the steeds, a shout from the men to clear the way, and a cheer from the bystanders.

Two of these bystanders started off alongside of the engine, with glittering eyes and flushed cheeks. The Bloater and Little Jim had heard the telegraph read off, had caught the words, "Fire—Saint Katharine's Docks," and knew well what that implied. They resolved to witness the fight, and ran as if their lives depended on the race. It need scarcely be said that the engine quickly left them out of sight behind, not only because the horses were fleet, but also because various pedestrians, into whose bosoms the boys plunged in their blind haste, treated them rather roughly, and retarded their progress a good deal. But nothing short of a knock-down blow could have put a full stop to the career of those imps of the broom. After innumerable hair-breadth escapes from "bobbies" and others, by agile bounds and desperate plunges among horses' legs and carriage-wheels, they reached the scene of action not *very* long after the engine with which they had set out.

It was night. The fire had been raging for some time with terrible fury, and had already got full possession of two large warehouses, each five or six floors in height, all connected by means of double iron folding-doors, and stored from basement to roof with spirits, tallow, palm-oil, cotton, flax, jute, and other merchandise, to the extent of upwards of two millions sterling in value. The dock fire-engines had been brought to bear on the flames a few minutes after the fire was discovered. The two floating-engines were paddled at once to the spot, and their powerful hydrants poured continuous streams on the flames; while, every few minutes, another and another of the land-engines came rattling up, until all the available force of the Red Brigade was on the spot, each man straining, like the hero of a forlorn hope, regardless of life and limb, to conquer the terrible foe. The Brompton and Chelsea volunteer fire-brigade, and several private engines, also came up to lend a helping hand. But all these engines, brave hearts, and vigorous proceedings, appeared at first of no avail, for the greedy flames shot out their tongues, hissed through water and steam, and licked up the rich fuel with a deep continuous roar, as if they gloated over their unusually splendid banquet, and meant to enjoy it to the full, despite man's utmost efforts to oppose them.

The excitement at this time was tremendous. Every available spot of ground or building from which the most limited view of the fire could be obtained, was crowded to excess by human beings, whose upturned faces were lighted more or less ruddily according to their distance from the fire.

No doubt the greater proportion of the vast multitude beheld the waste of so much property with anxiety and regret. Doubtless, also, many thoughtless ones were there who merely enjoyed the excitement, and looked on it as a pyrotechnic display of unwonted splendour. But there was yet another class of men, aye, and women, whose view of the matter was fitted to cause anxiety in the breasts of those who talk of "elevating the masses," and this was by far the largest class. The greater part of them belonged to the lowest class of labourers, men willing to work for their living, but who got little to do. Amongst these not one expression of regret was to be heard, though the women sometimes asked anxiously whether any one was likely to be hurt. But let a few of these speak for themselves.

"Ah," said an old woman, with an unintellectual style of countenance, "now there will be plenty of work for poor men."

"Yes," responded a rough, with a black eye, "that's true. My blissin', as Paddy says, on a fire; it warms the cockles o' yer heart an' kapes yer hands busy."

"They've much need to be kep' busy, sure enough," remarked another man, "for mine have been pretty idle for more than a week."

"I wish," exclaimed another, with a bitter curse on mankind in general, "that the whole Thames would go a-fire, from Westminster to Gravesend."

The energy with which this was said caused a general laugh and a good deal of chaff, but there was no humour in the man who spoke. He was one of those of whom it is said by a periodical which ought to know, that hundreds of such may be seen day by day, year by year, waiting at the different gates of the docks, in stolid weariness, for the chance of a day's work—the wage of which is half-a-crown. When a foreman comes to a gate to take on a few such hands, the press of men, and the faces, hungry and eager beyond description, make one of the saddest of the sad sights to be seen even at the east end of London.

In another part of the crowd, where the street was narrow, a scene of a most fearful kind was being enacted. All scoundreldom appeared to have collected in that spot. For two or three hours robbery and violence reigned unchecked in the very face of the police, who, reduced to inaction by the density of the crowd, could render little or no assistance to the sufferers. Scarcely one respectably dressed person was unmolested. Hats were indiscriminately smashed over the brows of their wearers, coats were torn off their backs, and watches and purses violently wrested from their owners. In many cases there was no attempt at secrecy, men were knocked down and plundered with all the coolness and deliberation with which we commonly pursue our lawful calling.

By degrees the perseverance and heroism of the firemen were rewarded. The fire began to succumb to the copious floods with which it was deluged, and, towards midnight, there was a perceptible diminution in the violence of the flames. There were, however, several temporary outbursts from time to time, which called for the utmost watchfulness and promptitude on the part of the Brigade.

During one of these a block of private dwellings nearest to the conflagration was set on fire. So intent was every one on the *great* fire that this incidental one was not observed until it had gained considerable headway. The buildings were very old and dry, so that, before an engine could be detached from the warehouses, it was in a complete blaze. Most of the inhabitants escaped by the chief staircase before it became impassable, and one or two leaped from the lower windows.

It chanced that Joe Dashwood's engine was nearest to this house at the time, and was run up to it.

"Now then, lads, look alive," said Joe, as the men affixed the hose and suction-pipe.

"Out o' the way!" cried Ned Crashington to two boys who appeared to be rather curious about the operations of the firemen.

"I say," exclaimed the Bloater in great excitement, "why—that's the 'ouse w'ere *Martha* lives!"

"Who's Martha?" asked Ned, without interrupting his operation of screwing on an additional length of hose.

"W'y, the friend o' Joe Dashwood's wife—Martha—Martha Reading, you know."

"Eh!" exclaimed Ned, looking up.

At that moment Martha herself appeared at a window in the upper storey, waving her arms and shrieking wildly for help. Men were seen endeavouring to bring forward a fire-escape, but the crowd was so dense as to render this an unusually difficult and slow operation.

Without uttering a word, Ned Crashington dashed up the blazing staircase. For a moment he was lost to view, but quickly reappeared, attempting to cross a half-charred beam which overhung a yawning gulf of fire where the first and second floors had just fallen in. Suddenly a dense mass of smoke surrounded him. He staggered, threw up his arms, and was seen to fall headlong into the flames. A deep groan, or cry of horror, arose from the crowd, and wild shouts of "fetch a ladder," "bring up the escape," were heard, while poor Martha got out on the window-sill to avoid the flames, which were rapidly drawing towards and almost scorching her.

Just then a man was seen to dash furiously through the crowd, he fought his way madly—knocking down all who opposed him. Gaining the door of the burning house he sprang in.

"I say," whispered Little Jim, in an excited voice, "it's Phil Sparks!"

"I'm glad to hear it," observed a quiet, broad-shouldered man, who stood near two policemen, to whom he winked knowingly.

The Bloater attempted to move off, but one of the policemen detained him. The other detained Little Jim.

Meanwhile the crowd looked for Phil's reappearance on the beam from which poor Ned Crashington had fallen, but Phil knew the house better than Ned. He gained the upper floor by a back stair, which was not quite impassable; seized Martha in his arms, just as she was about to leap into the street, and dragged her back into the smoke and flames. It appeared almost certain that both must have perished; but in a few seconds the man was seen to descend the lower stair with the woman in his arms, and in another moment a wild enthusiastic cheer burst from the vast multitude as he leaped into the street.

Laying Martha gently down on a doorstep, Sparks bent over her, and whispered in her ear. She appeared to have swooned, but opened her eyes, and gazed earnestly in the face of her deliverer.

"The Lord must have sent you to save me, Phil; He will save *you* also, if you will trust Him."

"Forgive me, Martha, I was hard on you, but—"

"God bless you, Phil—"

"Clear the way there," cried a commanding voice; "here, doctor, this way."

The crowd opened. A medical man came forward and examined Martha, and pronounced her to be only slightly injured. Several men then raised her and carried her towards a neighbouring house. Phil Sparks was about to follow, but the quiet man with the broad shoulders touched him gently on the arm, and said that he was "wanted."

"Sorry to interrupt you in such a good work, but it can't be helped. Other people can take care of her now, you know; come along."

Sparks' first impulse was to knock the quiet man down and fly, but he felt a restraining power on his other arm, and, looking round, observed a tall policeman at his side. As if by magic, another tall policeman appeared in front of him, and a third behind him. He suddenly bent down his head and suffered himself to be led away. Seeing this, the Bloater and Little Jim wrenched themselves from the grasp of their respective captors, dived between the legs of the bystanders, as eels might do among sedges, and vanished, to their own inexpressible delight and the total discomfiture of the "bobbies." They met a few minutes later at a well-known rendezvous.

"I wish 'e 'adn't bin took," said the Bloater with a look of regret on his expressive though dirty countenance.

"Poor Martha!" said Little Jim, almost crying as he thought of her. "'Ow much d'you think 'e'll get, Bloater?"

"Twenty years at least; p'r'aps go for life; you see it's an aggrawated case. I've bin makin' partikler inquiries, and I finds 'e's bin raisin' no end o' fires doorin' the last six months—kep' the Red Brigade trottin' about quite in a surprisin' way. I rather fear that 'e'll be let in for ever an' a day."

The Bloater was not quite correct in his guess. When the trial came on, to the surprise of all, especially of his "pals," Phil Sparks pleaded *guilty*! Partly in consideration of this, and partly on account of his last courageous act in saving the girl, he was let off with fifteen years penal servitude.

But, to return from this episode. The great fire at the docks, after gutting several warehouses, was finally subdued. And what of the loss? A hundred thousand pounds did not cover it, and every insurance office in London suffered! In addition to this, several persons lost their lives, while the Red Brigade, besides having some of their number more or less severely injured, lost one of its best and bravest men.

Gallant Ned Crashington's fighting days were over. His mangled remains were gathered up next morning, and, a few days later, were conveyed by his comrades to their last resting-place.

It is no easy matter to move the heart of London. That vast nation-in-a-city has too many diverse interests to permit of the eyes of all being turned, even for a moment, upon one thing. Nevertheless the fireman's funeral seemed to cause the great cord to vibrate for a little. Hundreds of thousands of people turned out to witness the cortège. Ned's coffin was drawn, military fashion, on one of the engines peculiar to his profession, with his helmet and hatchet placed upon the lid. The whole of the force of the brigade that could be spared followed him in uniform, headed by their chief, and accompanied by a large detachment of the police force. The procession was imposing, and the notices that appeared next day in all the papers were a touching tribute of respect to the self-sacrificing fireman, who, as one of these papers said, "left a widow and son, in poor circumstances, to mourn his early death."

Ah, these things were soon forgotten in the rush of the world's business by all save that widow and son, and one or two bosom friends. Even the men of the Red Brigade *appeared* to forget the fallen hero very soon. We say "appeared," because there were some among them who mourned Ned as a dear brother, chief among whom was Joe Dashwood. But whatever the feelings of the firemen might have been, theirs was a warfare that allowed no time for the undue indulgence or exhibition of grief. The regular "calls" and duties went on steadily, sternly, as if nothing had occurred, and before Ned's remains had lain a night in their last resting-place, many of his old comrades were out again doing fierce battle with the restless and untameable flames.

Chapter Nine.

Years passed away, and with them many old things vanished, while many novelties appeared, but the Red Brigade remained much as it was, excepting that it was, if possible, smarter and more energetic than ever.

In the lobby of our West-end station one pleasant summer evening, the men sat and stood about the open door beside the trim engines and *matériel* of their profession, chatting heartily as men are won't to do when in high health and spirits. There were new faces among them, but there were also several that had long been familiar there. The stalwart form of Joe Dashwood was there, so little altered by time that there was nothing about him to tell that he was passing the period of middle-age, save a few grey hairs that mingled here and there with the dark curls on his temples. Bob Clazie was there also, but he had not stood the trials of his profession so well as Joe—probably his constitution was not so strong. A disagreeable short cough harassed him, though he made light of it. Frequent scorching, smoking, and partial suffocation had increased his wrinkles and rendered his eyelids permanently red. Nevertheless, although nearly fifty years old, Bob Clazie was still one of the best men in the Brigade.

Joe Dashwood wore a pair of brass epaulettes on his shoulders, which indicated that he had attained to the highest rank in the service, short of the chief command.

He was giving directions to one of the younger men of the force, when a tall strapping young man, with a plain but open and singularly pleasing countenance entered, and going up to him shook him warmly by the hand.

"Well, Bob, what's the news? you seem excited this evening," said Joe.

"So I am, Joe; and with good reason too, for several pleasant things have happened to-day. In the first place, my friend and patron—"

"That's the old gentleman with the ruddy face and the bald head?" interrupted Joe.

"Yes, and with the kind heart. Don't ever omit the kind heart, Joe, in your description of him, else you'll only have painted half the portrait."

"Well, but the kind heart ain't quite so visible at first sight as the ruddy face and bald head, you know."

"Perhaps not; but if you watched him long enough to see him *act*, you'd perceive the kind heart as plain as if it hung at his button-hole, and beat like a sixty-horse-power steam-engine *outside* his ribs instead of inside," said the strapping young man with quite a glow of enthusiasm. "Oh, if you could only see how that old gentleman labours, and strives, and wears himself out, in his desire to rescue what they call our Street Arabs, you couldn't help loving him as I do. But I'm wandering from the pleasant things I've got to tell about. Through his influence my friend Jim has obtained a good appointment on the Metropolitan Railway, which gives him a much better salary than he had in Skrimp's office, and opens up a prospect of promotion; so, although it sends him underground before his natural time, he says he is quite content to be buried alive, especially as it makes the prospect of his union with a very small and exceedingly charming little girl with black eyes not quite so remote as it was. In the second place, you'll be glad to hear that the directors of the insurance office with which I am connected have raised my salary, influenced thereto by the same old gentleman with the ruddy face, bald head, and kind heart—"

"Coupled with your own merits, Bob," suggested Joe.

"I know nothing about *that*," replied the strapping young man with a smile, "but these pleasant pieces of good fortune have enabled me and Jim to carry out a plan which we have long cherished—to lodge together, with Martha Reading as our landlady. In truth, anticipating some such good fortune as has been sent to us, we had some time ago devoted part of our savings to the purpose of rescuing poor Martha from that miserable needlework which has been slowly killing her so long. We have taken and furnished a small house, Martha is already installed as the owner, and we go there to-night for the first time, as lodgers."

"You don't say so!" exclaimed Joe, laughing; "why, Bob, you and your friend act with as much promptitude as if you had been regularly trained in the Fire-Brigade."

"We received much of our training *from* it, if not *in* it," returned the strapping young man with the plain but pleasant countenance. "Don't you remember, Joe, how perseveringly we followed you in former days when *I* was the Bloater and *he* was Little Jim?"

"Remember it! I should think I do," replied Joe. "How glad my Mary will be when she hears what you have done."

"But that's not all my news," continued the Bloater, (if we may presume to use the old name). "Last, but not least, Fred has asked me to be his groom's-man. He wrote me a very pathetic letter about it, but omitted to mention the day—not to be wondered at in the circumstances. Poor Fred, his letter reminded me of the blotted copies which I used to write with such trouble and sorrow at the training school to which my patron sent me."

"There's reason for the blotted letter besides the excitement of his approaching marriage," said Joe. "He hurt his hand the last fire he attended, and it's in a sling just now, so he must have taken it out, for temporary duty when he wrote to you. The truth is that Fred is too reckless for a fireman. He's scarcely cool enough. But I can inform you as to the day; it is Thursday next. See that you are up to time, Bob."

"No fear of me being late," replied the Bloater. "By the way, have you heard of that new method of putting out fires that somebody has invented?"

"I did hear of some nonsensical plan," replied Joe, with a slight expression of contempt, "but I don't think it worth while to pay attention to things o' this sort. There's nothin' can beat good cold water."

"I'm not so sure of that, Joe," replied his friend gravely. "I have been reading an account of it in the *Insurance Guardian*, and it seems to me that there is something worth attending to in the new plan. It looks as if there was life in it, for a company is to be got up called the 'Fire and Water Company.'"

"But what *is* this new plan?" asked Joe, sending forth a violent puff from his pipe, as if to indicate that it would all end in smoke.

"Well, I'm not sure that I've got a correct notion of it myself, but my impression is that carbonic acid gas is the foundation-principle of it. Fire cannot exist in the presence of this gas—wherever it goes extinction of fire is instantaneous, which is more than you can say for water, Joe; for as you know well, fire, when strong enough, can turn that into steam as fast as you can pour it on, and after getting rid of it in this way, blaze up as furious as ever. What this company proposes to do is to saturate water with this carbonic acid gas mixed with nitrogen, and then pour that prepared water on fires. Of course, if much water were required, such a plan would never succeed, but a very small quantity is said to be sufficient. It seems that some testing experiments of a very satisfactory kind have been made recently—so you see, Joe, it is time to be looking out for a new profession!"

"H'm. I'll stick to the old brigade, at all events till the new company beats us from the field. Perhaps when that happens they'll enrol some of us to work the—what d'ye call 'em?—soda-water engines. They'll have engines of course, I suppose?"

"Of course," replied the Bloater; "moreover, they mean to turn their prepared water to good account when there are no fires to put out. It is said that the proportions of the mixture can be so varied that, with one kind, the pump may be used for the clarification of beer, oils, treacle, quicksilver, and such like, and for the preservation of fruit, meat, milk, etcetera, and with another mixture they propose to ventilate mines and tunnels; water gardens; kill insects on trees and flowers; soften water for domestic uses, and breweries, and manufacture soda-water, seltzer water, and other aerated beverages—"

"Oh, I say, Bob, hold on," cried Joe; "you seem to forget that my capacity for swallowing is limited."

"Well, perhaps you'll get it enlarged enough before long, to swallow all that and a deal more," said the Bloater, with a half serious air. "Meanwhile I'll continue to wish all success and prosperity to the Red Brigade—though you *do* cause a tremendous amount of damage by your floods of water, as we poor insurance companies know. Why, if it were not for the heroes of the salvage corps we should be ruined altogether. It's my opinion, Joe, that the men of the salvage corps run quite as much risk as your fellows do in going through fire and smoke and working among falling beams and tumbling walls in order to cover goods with their tarpaulins and protect them from water."

"I admit that the salvage men do their work like heroes," said Joe; "but if you would read our chief's report for last year, you would see that we do our best to put out fires with the smallest possible amount of water. Why, we only used about eleven million gallons in the last twelve months—a most insignificant quantity that, for the amount of work done!"

A tinkle of the telegraph bell here cut short the conversation. "Fire, in the Mall, Kensington," was the signal.

"Get her out, lads!" cried Joe, referring to the engine.

Helmets and hatchets were donned and buckled on in the old style, and quiet jokes or humorous and free-and-easy remarks were uttered in slow, even sleepy tones, while the men acted with a degree of prompt celerity that could not have been excelled had their own lives depended on their speed. In three minutes, as usual, they were off at full gallop. The Bloater—who still longed to follow them as of old, but had other business on hand—wished them "good luck," and proceeded at a smart pace to his new lodgings.

We must change the scene now, for the men of the Red Brigade do not confine their attentions exclusively to such matters as drilling, fighting, suffering, conquering, and dying. They sometimes marry! Let us look in at this little church where, as a passer-by remarks, "*something* appears to be going on."

A tall handsome young man leads to the altar a delicate, beautiful, blooming bride, whose bent head and blushing cheek, and modest mien and dependent air, contrast pleasantly with the gladsome firm countenance, stalwart frame, and self-reliant aspect of the bridegroom.

Looking at them as they stood then, no one could have entertained for a moment the idea that these two had ever united in the desperate and strenuous attempt to put out a fire! Yet so it was. They had, once upon a time, devoted themselves to the extinction of a fire in a cupboard with such enthusiasm that they had been successful not only in putting that fire out, but in lighting another fire, which nothing short of union for life could extinguish!

Joe Dashwood gave away the bride, and he could not help remarking in a whisper to the Bloater, (who was also there in sumptuous attire), that if ever a man was the born image of his father that man was Fred Crashington—an opinion which was heartily responded to by Mrs Maggie Crashington, who, then in the period of life which is described as "fat, fair, and forty," looked on at the proceedings with intense satisfaction. Mary Dashwood—also fat, fair, and forty—was there too, and if ever a woman congratulated herself on a rosebud having grown into a full blown blush-rose, that woman was Mary.

Besides a pretty large company of well-dressed people, with white favours in their breasts, there was a sprinkling of active men with sailor-like caps, who hung about the outskirts of the crowd, and among these were two or three stout fellows with brass helmets and dirty hands and faces, and wet garments, who had returned from a recent fire just in time to take a look at their comrade and his fair bride.

"Poor Ned, how his kind heart would have rejoiced to see this day!" murmured Joe, brushing his cheek hastily as he retired from the altar.

So, the wedding party left the church, and the firemen returned to their posts of watchfulness and duty.

About the same period that this wedding took place, there was another wedding in the great metropolis to which we would draw the reader's attention. Not that it was a great one or a splendid one; on the contrary, if it was marked by any unusual peculiarities, these were shabbiness and poverty. The wedding party consisted of only two, besides the bride and bridegroom, and everything was conducted with such quietness, and gravity, and absence of excitement, that it might almost have been mistaken for a funeral on a small scale by any one unacquainted with the ceremonial appertaining thereto.

The happy pair, besides looking very sad, were past the meridian of life. Both were plainly dressed, and each appeared desirous of avoiding observation. The man, in particular, hung his head and moved awkwardly, as if begging forgiveness generally for presuming to appear in the character of a bridegroom. His countenance had evidently never been handsome, but there was a sad subdued look about it—the result, perhaps, of prolonged suffering—which prevented it from being repulsive. He looked somewhat like an invalid, yet his powerful frame and the action of his strong muscular hands were not in keeping with that idea.

The bride, although careworn and middle-aged, possessed a singularly sweet and attractive countenance—all the more attractive that it wore a habitual expression of sadness. It was a sympathetic face, too, because it was the index to a loving, sympathetic, Christian soul, and its ever-varying indications of feeling, lightened and subdued and modified, but never quite removed, the sadness.

The two who composed the remainder of this wedding party were young men, apparently in a higher position of life than the principals. The one was tall and strapping, the other rather small, but remarkably active and handsome. It was evident that they were deeply interested in the ceremony in which they took part, and the smaller of the two appeared to enjoy some humorous reminiscences occasionally, to judge from the expression of his face when his glance chanced to meet that of his tall friend.

As they were leaving the altar, the bridegroom bent down and murmured in a deep soft voice—

"It's like a dream, Martha. It ain't easy to believe that such good luck should come to the likes o' me."

The bride whispered something in reply, which was inaudible to those who followed.

"Yes, Martha, yes," returned the bridegroom; "no doubt it is as you put it. But after all, there's only one of His sayin's that has gone right home to me. I've got it by heart *now*—'I came not to call the righteous, but *sinners* to repentance.' 'Twould have bin all up with me long ago but for that, Martha."

They reached the door at this point, got into a cab, and drove away. The remainder of the wedding party left the little church on foot.

The same evening on which this event took place, the strapping young man and the little active youth sat together at the open window of a comfortable though small parlour, enjoying a cup of tea. The view from the window was limited, but it possessed the charm of variety; commanding as it did, a vista of chimney-pots of every shape and form conceivable—many of which were capped with those multiform and hideous contrivances with which foolish man vainly endeavours to cure smoke.

"Well, Jim," asked the strapping youth, as he gazed pensively on this prospect, "what d'you think of it?"

"What do you refer to, Bob—our view or the wedding?"

"The wedding, of course."

"It's hard to say," replied Jim, musing. "He seemed to be such an unmitigated scoundrel when we first made his acquaintance that it is difficult to believe he is a changed man now."

"By which you mean to insinuate, Jim, that the Gospel is not sufficient for out-and-out blackguards; that it is only powerful enough to deal with such modified scoundrels as you and I were."

"By no means," replied Jim, with a peculiar smile; "but, d'you know, Bloater, I never can feel that we were such desperate villains as you make us out to have been, when we swept the streets together."

"Just listen to him!" exclaimed the Bloater, smiting his knee with his fist, "you can't *feel*!—what have *feelings* to do with knowledge? Don't you *know* that we were fairly and almost hopelessly *in the current*, and that we should probably have been swept off the face of the earth by this time if it had not been for that old gentleman with the bald head and the kindly—"

"There, now, Bloater, don't let us have any more of that, you become positively rabid when you get upon that old gentleman, and you are conceited enough, also, to suppose that all the gratitude in the world has been shovelled into your own bosom. Come, let us return to the point, what do I think of the wedding—well, I think a good deal of it. There is risk, no doubt, but there is that in everything sublunary. I think, moreover, that the marriage is founded on *true love*. He never would have come to his present condition but for true love to Martha, which, in God's providence, seems to have been made the means of opening his mind to Martha's *message*, the pith of which message was contained in his last remark on leaving the church. Then, as to Martha, our own knowledge of her would be sufficient to ease our minds as to her wisdom, even if it were not coupled with the reply she made to me when I expressed wonder that she should desire to marry such a man. 'Many waters,' she said, 'cannot quench love!'"

"Ha! you know something of that yourself," remarked Bob with a smile.

"Something," replied Little Jim, with a sigh.

"Well, don't despond," said the Bloater, laying his hand on Jim's shoulder. "I have reason to know that the obstacles in your way shall soon be removed, because that dear old gentleman with the—"

He was cut short by a loud, gruff shouting in the street below, accompanied by the rattling of wheels and the clatter of horses' hoofs.

"Ah, there they go!" cried Jim, his eyes glistening with enthusiasm as he and his friend leaned out of the window, and strove to gain a glimpse of the street between the forest of chimneys, "driving along, hammer and tongs, neck or nothing, always at it night and day. A blessing on them!"

"Amen," said the Bloater, as he and Jim resumed their seats and listened to the sound of the wheels, voices, and hoofs dying away in the distance.

Reader, we re-echo the sentiment, and close our tale with the remark that there are many rescued men and women in London who shall have cause, as long as life shall last, to pray for a blessing on the overwrought heroes who fill the ranks, and fight the battles of the Red Brigade.

| Chapter 1 | | Chapter 2 | | Chapter 3 | | Chapter 4 | | Chapter 5 | | Chapter 6 | | Chapter 7 | | Chapter 8 | | Chapter 9 |